Pressing On...

(Perseverance until Deliverance)

Dennis Jones

Philippians 3:14
"I press toward the mark for the prize of
the high calling of God in Christ Jesus."

authorHOUSE®

AuthorHouse™
1663 Liberty Drive
Bloomington, IN 47403
www.authorhouse.com
Phone: 1-800-839-8640

First published by AuthorHouse 5/6/2011

ISBN: 978-1-4520-2040-2 (e)
ISBN: 978-1-4520-2038-9 (sc)
ISBN: 978-1-4520-2039-6 (hc)

Library of Congress Control Number: 2010912389

Printed in the United States of America

This book is printed on acid-free paper.

DEDICATION

†

There were many times while writing this book that I felt discouraged. My loving wife and three adult children encouraged me to continue on. The support they have shown while preparing this book has been overwhelming. Their love for me has been unending and for that I would like to dedicate this book to each one of them.

I would like to extend a special thanks to my wife, Donna, for her part in this book. She not only endured great hardship during my recovery process, but she was able to put her experiences in writing for this book. It was a hard chapter for me to read, but an important dose of reality. You will find her story in Chapter Four. It is my prayer that her story will help encourage others to press on.

ACKNOWLEDGMENTS

✝

I would like to thank my Pastor, Bill Kellough, for his kind words in writing the Foreword for this book. His example through his relationship with Jesus Christ has encouraged me to strive for a stronger relationship with Christ in my life.

I would like to thank my friend and the Educational Pastor of my church, Tim Garrett. He helped me finalize the biblical context in this book. His instruction has helped bring this book to a level that is honoring to Christ.

I also would like to thank my sister, Teresa Mossberger, the photographer that took the pictures for this book. She was a huge encouragement while writing this book.

I finally would like to thank those that helped me edit this book. I would like to thank my dad, David Jones, as well as two close friends of the family, Julie Greenbank and Joanne McGarrh. Together they have developed this book into a tool the Holy Spirit of God can use to change lives.

CONTENTS

FOREWORD

†

How in the world can a person mess his life up so badly? When you discover yourself on the bottom, manipulated and controlled by lusts, cravings, greed, vices or unwholesome companions and circumstances, is there any hope? I suppose we have all asked at one time or the other; can anybody be as evil in mind and heart as I am? Well, the Bible brings clarity to these questions. We are all made out of the same stuff. All have sinned; there is none good, no not one. The apostle Paul said that "**. . . all our righteousnesses are as filthy rags;" (Isaiah 64:6).** Every member of the human race stands before a Holy God, condemned and worthy of His judgment. But, the wonderful thing is that this Holy God, who is our creator, is also a God of love who is rich in mercy and grace. **"For God so loved the world, that He gave His only begotten Son, that whosoever believeth in Him should not perish, but have everlasting life" (John 3:16).**

This book contains the personal story of Dennis Jones, who is a trophy of God's Grace in the making. I have been Dennis' and his wife's pastor since 1990. As I read his manuscript I experienced a range of emotions from sadness and tears to joy and rejoicing. Though I have considered myself very involved in the life of this author and his family, I became aware of many of their feelings and thoughts that I was oblivious of. I see my own shortcomings in being there for him and his family at some times of great need in this twenty year journey. For this I humbly apologize both for myself and my people.

Dennis recounts the story of his life in a very humble, honest and forthright way. Though he could probably point fingers at others and their influence on what he became, he takes full and personal responsibility for himself. He is somewhat like David of the Old Testament who after his tragic fall into sin with Bethsheba, the murder of her husband to try to cover up his sin and finally the death of his baby, in heartsickness, sorrow and repentance cried out to God and confessed **"Against thee, thee only, have I sinned," (Psalms 51:4)**. The life of Dennis has been a series of up's and down's. He has had to pay a heavy price for some bad choices and is still paying the price. He also has been the recipient of God's marvelous grace and knows the joy of being an over comer.

You will learn a great deal by reading this book and hopefully, you will be encouraged to delve deeper into a personal faith relationship with Christ Jesus our Lord and experience the abundant life found in Him that frees you from the shackles that enslaves mankind.

~ Rev. Bill Kellough

PREFACE

†

    This is an autobiography of my life, in which I have shared different segments of time in order to reach out to those who may relate to my experiences. The idea of this book was heavy on my heart for a few years, due to the continued reports of sexual abuse that has been broadcast around our country. The reality that the total number of registered sex offenders in this nation has increased to staggering numbers, beckons for someone to try something to reverse this frightening trend. It is clear that the effects of sexual abuse have swept through our country harming many generations, leaving many innocent victims along the way. It is my goal to create a tool that the Holy Spirit of God can use to change the wicked hearts of those caught in this web of immorality.

    It is my intent to utilize this book as such a tool to reach out to every sex offender in this county. I understand personally the power of sexual immoralities as well as the various consequences created by falling to these kinds of temptations. I was on the sex offender registry in the state of Indiana for a total of 14 years, giving me firsthand knowledge of its consequences. I hope to utilize my experiences to help those that can be helped. It will be God's Holy Spirit who will ultimately determine who can and will be helped. This book is just one tool that can be used to expose the need for help.

My focus through this book is to share how I was freed from the bondage of sexual immorality. I try to describe to the reader how the Lord Jesus worked in my heart and life, using the wisdom of His Word to help me re-direct the choices I made on a daily basis. I was changed both mentally and spiritually, and I have complete faith that the Lord can also change others who have been overtaken in sexual immorality. This change is laid out in detail in hopes that those affected will learn from my mistakes in order to deter them from making the same mistakes.

This book breaks open the Word of God, utilizing scripture to reveal truths that can change lives. I concede that I am not an ordained minister; that is why my biblical studies for this book have been reviewed and approved by the educational pastors of my church. I understand that true and lasting change must not just come from psychological counseling, but also from the Holy Spirit using God's Word to penetrate our heart and mind. Knowing firsthand how my life has been changed gives me no doubt that many more lives will be transformed. The intent of this book is to use what the Lord has taught me through His Word and the working of His Spirit to make every attempt to help change the lives of others, which ultimately will be through the power of God's Word and the Holy Spirit.

INTRODUCTION

✝

In the process of writing this book I have been asked, "Why do you want to reach the sex offenders of this country?" I see sin as sin regardless of its level of impact on society. It is clear that sins have different consequences, but over-all sin deserves death. **"For the wages of sin is death; but the gift of God is eternal life through Jesus Christ our Lord" (Romans 6:23).** It is that gift in Jesus Christ that I wish to share with everyone that reads this book. **"And He is the propitiation for our sins: and not for ours only, but also for the sins of the whole world" (I John 2:2).** I sincerely believe that through the awesome grace of God in Jesus Christ that lives can be forever changed. I have experienced the grace of God. I know how it can impact you. When the taste of God's forgiveness and liberating grace has been experienced, that person is changed for life.

This book points out that the acts committed by sex offenders are not all cases stemming from mental illness. There are many that are dealing with the sinful desires of their flesh. It is my belief that they can still be transformed both mentally and spiritually. When dealing with these individuals, it is important to call these acts what they are, which is sin. This thought is not new; the Word of God supports this completely. **"For when we were in the flesh, the motions of sins, which were by the law, did work in our members to bring forth fruit unto death" (Romans 7:5).** Calling their behavior an illness leaves the offender with little hope for recovery, considering their fate is left in the hands of man trying to reach them through secular counseling and medication. Calling their behavior what it is, which is sin leaves the offender in need of a Savior. **"When Jesus heard it, He saith unto them, they that are whole have no need of the physician, but they that are sick: I came not to call the righteous, but sinners to repentance" (Mark 2:17).**

I do want to point out that I recognize the level of depravity in this country. There are individuals in our society and in our penal institutions that have minds that have been consumed with their depravity; therefore, their hearts have been hardened against God. **"And even as they did not like to retain God in their knowledge, God gave them over to a reprobate mind, to do those things which are not convenient" (Romans 1:28).** The reality is that there are those that will not change. They do have a psychologically engrained preference toward sexual crimes. Therefore, it's reasonable to say they do have a mental illness. This justifies the need to maintain the nations sex offenders' registries. The complexity of separating those who have the possibility of being reformed from those who have been turned over to their reprobate minds explains the reasoning why all sex offenders are swept up with the same broom, although it does not justify it.

I have chosen to extend this book to all offenders trusting those that the Lord can reach will be touched by the power of the Holy Spirit through faith. If this book changes lives and in some small way stops the cycle of perversion that has been passed from generation to generation, then every second I spent writing it will have been worth it.

Ch. 1

†

HEARTACHE AND CONFUSION

It is hard to imagine the pain endured by those individuals who are living as victims of sexual crimes. The heartache caused by these crimes can be deep and long lasting. I know this because I became a victim of this crime at the age of eight. I experienced firsthand this heartache and confusion. There are many feelings that can overwhelm a victim: guilt, shame, anger, bitterness and loneliness. I have experienced all of these emotions and then some. I think it's important for everyone to understand the cycle of events that can occur in the life of a victim dealing with sexual abuse. This is why I wrote this book about my experiences, because I have come full circle in my life concerning this ordeal. I trust that my experiences will encourage those that have been victimized to push on toward a full life. I also hope that my experiences will encourage any victimizers reading this book to seek the help required to truly change their behavior.

According to the American Academy of Experts in Traumatic Stress, a very high degree of psychological damage can occur if the offender makes the victim feel physical pleasure during the offence(s). This will produce a level of guilt and shame that is very powerful. Moreover, the victim is less likely to disclose the abuse, and if he or she does, they are very likely to minimize it. This would be because the victim may feel partly to blame for the abuse because they experienced pleasure (this is a grooming technique). Countless victims who, after the abuse was revealed (either through someone observing, or indirectly), did not disclose the full extent. They fear they will get in trouble for not reporting it themselves, and further experience fear and shame because they experienced physical pleasure. As the victims grow older, they may be unable to process the abuse, and continue to blame both themselves as well as the offender. The shame produced can be so intense as to create a loss of self and self-destructive behaviors. Victims of child sexual abuse can go on to lead normal, healthy lives. They can learn to let go of the pain, and to increase their self-awareness of how the abuse affected them. Sometimes it takes the right therapist, the right book, or even just time. (http://www.aaets.org/article123.htm) [1.]

The reality that some victims become unable to process the abuse they experienced is why I strongly believe so many victims become victimizers. Many victims of sexual abuse harden themselves from the abuse they endured. This leads them to never receiving any type of counseling on how to deal with the effects of their abuse. Therefore, many victims of sexual crimes from America's past are now listed among the many registered sex offenders in America's present. The victims of past generations are now victimizing the current generation. This raises one of the greatest debates of our times. Is it possible to rehabilitate an offender from their sexual depravity? It is my experience that with proper Biblical and psychological counseling an offender can be restored to a useful place in society. I have learned firsthand that the Bible deals with both the mind and spirit of a person, which is required to overcome sexual addictions. This is something secular counseling does not offer or acknowledge.

There is a false perception that victims of sexual abuses are always traumatized by the abuse and therefore they must harbor bitterness and anger with the offender. This is not always the case. I was victimized by two separate individuals. One experience was by a close trusted family member whom, to this day, I love very much. This abuse did bring on many confused feelings including anger, but my love for this individual eased my anger. Therefore, I had no desire to report the abuse. I did not want to see this individual get into trouble.

The second offence I experienced was from a friend of my family. She was in her early thirties and very friendly to me. I was around the age of twelve and I think it's safe to say that I had a crush on her. By the time the abuse started, I was genuinely excited. I looked forward to the attention I received from her. I did not see her actions as abuse. I simply thought it was part of our relationship. Her actions toward me were subtle and gentle, making it seem right. I was never placed in any physical danger, nor did I feel threatened. The attention I received from her was welcomed, but at the same time the exposure I received through my experiences with her was premature. We never had sexual intercourse, but my experiences with her developed in me sexual fantasies that influenced my involvement with pornography.

This addiction was easy to feed around my house. My step-dad had a personal box of videos and magazines which was easy for me to get my hands on. After my parents went to bed, I would sneak downstairs to watch movies that filled my mind with sexual fantasies. I would sneak magazines up to my room to soak my mind with their images. It was not long before I got caught with my hand in the cookie jar. Instead of taking action to get me the help I needed to overcome my apparent addiction, my step-dad gave me the box of magazines. I celebrated by hanging my favorite pictures all over my wall like wallpaper. This only threw more fire on my inner turmoil. I hungered to experience the fantasies I witnessed both on video and in ink. But, despite my past abuses and sexually active imagination I was still a virgin. I had plenty of friends, and I had plenty of opportunities to have sex at the many parties I went to. Something in me wanted to save that part of my life with someone special. I really can't explain why. I did not have a spiritual upbringing. I had this void in my heart that simply was not filled by any girl I met, so I chose not to take our relationship to that level.

This void in my heart was troubling to me. I felt as if I was never going to meet anyone who could fill it. I did not believe that I had anyone to talk to about what I was going through. I understand the desire of wanting help as a child while at the same time being unable to talk about my experiences with anyone due to the confusion the experiences created. Since I chose to remain silent about my being victimized, I never received the proper counseling I so desperately needed. By the time I reached my teen years, I found myself totally obsessed with sexual fantasies. I was using drugs or alcohol on a daily basis. I was totally engulfed in pornography and the temptations surrounding that life style. In the midst of all this, I would find myself lying alone at night crying in loneliness. There was something missing in my life. I simply had no idea what it was. I knew I needed help, but I did not know how to tell anyone.

The confusion and turmoil that was going on in my heart was becoming too much for me to handle. I thought running away would help, but I didn't have anywhere to go. I chose then to contact my dad. I asked him if I could move in with him permanently. I did not fully share why I wanted to move in. I had no need to. He was more than happy to take me in. I should have taken that step a long time ago. I could not help but to think how much I could have avoided if I would have made this choice years earlier.

Life at my dad's house was completely different. The vices that seemed to control the behavior of everyone at my mom's house was not there. They had something there that I was not use to—RULES! That took some getting used to. I liked my freedom. But, I can say that during this period of my life I did not watch pornography either in magazines or movies, at least for awhile. Unfortunately, my mind was so filled with those images that I had plenty of dreams. This provoked my wicked imaginations to come back and ultimately exposed that void in my heart again. I was so happy at my dad's, but at the same time I hated myself for who I felt I was. I would visit my mother and every chance I could I would sneak a magazine out the door and hide it in my bedroom at my dad's. My step-mom was a very detailed lady, so I had to hide them carefully or she would find them. I did not want my dad to know what I was dealing with out of embarrassment. This only made that void in my heart larger making me even more reclusive.

Shortly thereafter I met a girl named Donna that I truly cared about. She related so well to me. I recall walking four miles every night to her house. I found that she met more than my sexual need. She related to me in so many other ways and our child hoods were very similar. I finally found someone I could open up to. We would talk for hours about everything we could think of. Both of us had baggage from our past, and we found that baggage to be lighter when we carried it together. This was the first time in my life that I ever experienced that kind of love. I knew that we were meant to be together and I wanted with all my heart to spend the rest of my life with her.

I will never forget the second date we had together when she introduced me to her daughter. I was clearly taken aback, but not detoured from my desire to know more about them both. It was not long until her daughter was calling me "Daddy Dennis". Her biological father ran off to Florida and chose not to meet his responsibility. This gave me a new sense of being needed. It was a welcomed emotion giving me a sense of purpose in my life. I found that caring about them both was very healing for me. It moved my focus off all the things that were troubling me. Around this time, I was a junior in high school so I could only see them at night. But, that did not prevent me from making sure I was there every evening. The love I felt for my new girlfriend was amazing. I felt at that point in my life that no one could love her as much as I did. Whatever it took for me to get there, I would do it. I remember asking my dad for rides to her house telling him it was a friend's house. When he asked my friend's name, I would give him Donna's brother's name. I am glad he never asked to meet him because he was seldom there.

My girlfriend, Donna and I shared a very addictive nature with drugs and alcohol. Both of our mothers smoked marijuana with us which we thought was cool. Our drug use, without a doubt, heightened our sexual experiences which only fed my addiction to sex even more. Needless to say, I lost my virginity during this stage of my life. The reality that both of our parents gave us too much freedom allowed us to spend a lot of time together. It wasn't long until we found out that Donna was pregnant with my child. My girlfriend's mother was not about to financially care for two grandchildren. I found myself in an interesting situation. Thankfully, I had nine months to work something out.

I still remember breaking the news to my dad. He actually guessed what I was going to say before I even had to tell him. He was clearly disappointed that I chose the path I was on. He proceeded to give me a lecture that any dad would give their son in this situation. I could not help but to think how much he did not know about me. I realized this was due to my hiding everything from him which I thought was best. Otherwise, I would have had my time with my girlfriend monitored. It was clear at that moment that my hiding things from him were over. However, I found this to be a positive thing because at that point in my life I really needed him. I was faced with the reality that I now had a family to support even though I did not have any means of income.

It was during this time that I realized how valuable the influence of my dad was in my life. He always gave me a strong example of being a hard worker. He showed me through his life that it is important to own up to your responsibility. This is why I decided to finish high school by taking night classes. Doing this freed me up to find a full time job to support my family. We didn't own a vehicle, so I had to ride my bicycle to work and take the evening school bus to school. We lived in a small rented apartment which cost us $85/wk. It was at one time a mortuary. Our bedroom had a window in the ceiling over our bed which, in the past, was used to keep the bodies in the mortuary at room temperature. It was a modest apartment that met our needs.

Although I worked hard to provide for my new family, I still found myself dealing with many personal issues. The example of my father was beneficial to me, but being raised in a divorced home since I was eight months old opened the door for a lot of negative influences. My mother and step-father were heavily involved in drugs and were very open about it. This influence taught me how to deal in illegal drugs. I used this knowledge to help us pay the bills. I recall both my mother and step-father living with us for a short period during this time. It was like a daily party while they were there. I always hid this lifestyle from my dad. I did not want him to know that side of my life. It was not difficult for me to hide this from my dad; I was brought up from childhood to hide things of this nature from him. As a child, I use to think it was to protect his feelings, but as I grew up it became apparent that it was to protect the lifestyle we all wished to maintain.

It was not long after the birth of our son that my dad offered to allow my family to move into one of his apartments. We jumped on that offer, knowing that it would be much better living quarters for the children. Then, a local church stopped by our apartment to invite our four year old daughter to Vacation Bible School. The following Sunday they invited us to church. Donna had agreed to attend. At that time, I didn't want anything to do with church. It was during her time in church that she had met another man who loved her even more than I. When she returned home, all she talked about for two days was Jesus Christ and how she trusted Him as her Savior.

During those two days, I witnessed a new sense of hope in Donna's life to which she credited to her new relationship with Christ. That is about the time when the church pastor and a deacon stopped by our apartment to share the gospel with me. That is the day I was introduced to Jesus Christ. I still recall stating to the pastor, "Whatever it is she has, I want it." The change that had taken place in Donna's outlook on life was very apparent to me. She seemed happier then I had ever seen her. I realized that day that Christ died for my sins, too. That was the day I accepted Christ as my personal Savior. It was at this moment that both my girlfriend and I realized that we no longer had to carry the baggage of our past. When we asked Christ to be our Lord and Savior, we laid all that baggage at His feet. We began learning to live for Christ which at first seemed easy. However, the influences of those around us were very strong. It wasn't always easy saying no. We literally had to avoid many of our old friends and family members for quite a long time.

I will get into the process of cleaning up our lives in the next chapter, but one thing I learned is that being set apart unto Christ is a process of spiritual growth. This process did not occur immediately for us as I thought it would. It was a daily choice in surrendering to His Word. Before long, both my girlfriend and I realized we needed to get married so, we sought the help of the church and had a glorious Cinderella wedding. The youth pastor's wife allowed Donna to wear her wedding dress. My sister had all the flowers made. My mother baked and decorated our wedding cake. My cousin took all the pictures. The church youth pastor sang the special music and the church pastor gladly married us. If it wasn't for the love of both our church and family, our special wedding day would have turned out much differently.

We walked faithfully for a few years serving in many areas within the church. We worked in the bus ministry, the youth group, and the children's ministry. It was during one summer at youth camp as a counselor that I felt the calling of the Lord in my life to preach His Word to the lost. I then began to preach during special services at church, in nursing homes and in the community homeless shelter. I began learning different magic tricks and how to become a ventriloquist all in order to be able to be used by the Lord more. My ministry at the church grew to the extent that I was neglecting my family. I didn't realize that in my absence my wife was slipping further and further away from both the Lord and me. I didn't know my wife was dealing with health issues that were dragging her down. In my ignorance, I failed to recognize that my first ministry was to my family. My new Christian walk was filled with a lot of zeal but little knowledge.

My inability to properly balance and manage my responsibilities brought on times of trial for Donna and I. Between my ignorance and Donna's battle with Cerebral Palsy; this added a lot of pressure to our relationship. As she became more ill and unable to meet all the needs I had, I felt a battle raging within my flesh. I should have fallen on my knees in prayer. I reverted back to the things that comforted me in my youth; the seeds of lust through pornography that I had planted deep within my heart and mind from years before began to grow again. I was unaware of its destruction. I found myself leaning on its comfort by yielding to the temptations I had raging in my flesh. I felt as if I never accepted Christ as my Savior. I was at war with myself as my flesh hungered for the lust that was in both my heart and mind. The Spirit living in me constantly beckoned me to turn back to Christ. I would find myself crying to the Lord for forgiveness. My grief and sorrow were real. I would destroy any pornography that I had in my possession to prove my repentant heart. Time after time, I would find myself yielding to my flesh once again which caused me to go out and simply purchase more pornography.

I recall going to my youth pastor crying that I felt like I was not a Christian. Together we drove to the senior pastor's home to further discuss the issue. The senior pastor sat with me and listened as I shared with him my fears of not ever accepting Christ. He then asked the question that to this day rings in my head. "Are you in sin?" I was set back by this question. I replied out of pride with a quick, "No". That response was the beginning of my destruction which is why to this day that response rings in my head. I should have been honest with my pastor. I know he could have helped me through God's Word. It's clear to me now that I just didn't want to let go of my sinful behavior.

It wasn't long after that night that I found my heart and mind overtaken in my sinful behavior. The only way I was going to turn from the path I found myself on was for my sins to be exposed. Through a series of events, that is exactly what occurred. My life as I knew it was over. I single handedly dismantled it. I devastated the ones I loved both friends and family. I demolished my Christian testimony and destroyed my usefulness to Christ. I was at the bottom of the barrel where sin ultimately takes you. There was only one thing I could do, and that was to look up. I was deeply sorry for the emotional pain I brought to my victim, my family and friends. I was even more remorseful for the open acts of sin that I committed before the Lord. I immediately sought forgiveness by repenting to the Lord and then openly asking for forgiveness to everyone involved. Donna and I immediately began counseling with the church pastor both for our marriage and to deal with the issues from my past.

Regardless of my state of repentance, there was a price to pay for my actions. It was not long before my sins were exposed to the authorities. I was quickly brought in for questioning in regards to what I had done. I sat there during all those questions faced with the reality that I was now a victimizer. Although my actions never led to physical contact, the pain I caused mentally will be long lasting to my victim. I was deeply sorry for what I had done and I didn't want to create any further hardship for anyone. I decided to accept the plea agreement offered by the state prosecutor. I placed my fate in the hands of the judge trusting that whatever I was dealt would be within the Lord's will. I was sentenced to one year in jail with one and a half years on probation. I was also ordered to serve ten years on the Indiana Sex Offender Registry.

I was a registered sex offender who had also been offended. I have experienced the deep heartache and confusion of being sexually molested as a child. I experienced the heartache and anguish of knowing I repeated the cycle. That grief was very overwhelming to me. I truly hated myself. I had to deal with the guilt and shame of turning from a victim to a victimizer. I had to experience the burden of seeking forgiveness than receiving it only to lose everything anyway. I lost my family, my job, my car, my Christian testimony and the different ministries I served within the church. All of this was lost due to my being overtaken by sin.

Upon my release after 10 months in jail, I experienced the embarrassing moments of people being shocked by viewing my information on the Indiana Sex Offender Registry. I endured the overwhelming feeling of anxiety every time the news would randomly flash pictures from the registry website on their evening broadcast. I had to learn how to survive in the work force, while knowing everyone knew about my past offenses. Worst of all, I had to witness the heartaches endured by my family due to the consequences brought on by my criminal conviction. They had to endure the embarrassing moments of being asked about my past by both friends and neighbors. My family had to live on limited income because I was not there for them. They had to learn to press forward in order to live their lives without me.

I am personally determined to use these experiences to help me grow spiritually, emotionally and intellectually. Accepting responsibility for my actions, I realize that all my experiences were consequences of my sinful behavior. Now, I wish to pass on my experiences and the experiences of my family in the hope of helping others. I hope that by sharing our story we can help break the chain of pain and suffering that is being passed on from one generation to another.

I have heard that a wise man learns from his mistakes, but an even wiser man learns from the mistakes of others. My prayer is that many will read this book and will be led to seek help with whatever struggles they are dealing with. It is important to make the choice to talk about these issues regardless if you are an individual dealing with the pains of being a sexual victim or a victimizer.

Ch. 2

†

CLEAN UP YOUR LIFE

I know from personal experiences that cleaning up your life is a day to day battle. This battle can be a positive endeavor if it is evidence that the one experiencing the battle has not given into their flesh. **"For the flesh lusteth against the Spirit, and the Spirit against the flesh: and these are contrary the one to the other: so that ye cannot do the things that ye would" (Galatians 5:17).** This battle is like having two dogs deep within your soul fighting one another for complete control. My pastor explained this fight between the flesh and the Spirit as two dogs fighting one another. He stated that whichever dog we feed the most would win the fight. This means that the fight can be won by either dog. If we yield to our flesh, the "bad dog" will win. If we yield to the Spirit of Christ, the "good dog" will win. I was just thankful that I had a "good dog" in the fight, because I can remember a time when that was not the case.

Thinking back to my youth, when I only had one dog in the fight, I was totally engulfed in the things of my flesh. I could do pretty much anything I wanted to without a second thought. That all changed on August 21st, 1990 the day the Holy Spirit revealed to me my need for Christ and opened my heart so I could accept Jesus Christ as my Savior. This is the day that changed my life forever and the day the Holy Spirit entered my life and began helping me fight against my flesh. As a new Christian, I was a bold follower of Christ. I would devour the Words of Christ on a daily basis. It was not long until I noticed that the "bad dog" within me was finally quiet. My personal passion and desire was completely yielded to the cause of Christ. I was serving a higher power than that of myself. I served Jesus Christ. Many older Christians call this period in a new believer's life the honeymoon period. I strongly believe this experience with Christ does not have to be limited to the period during your early walk with Christ. As individuals, we can choose to yield our lives to Christ daily and in so doing grow into a strong lasting relationship with Jesus Christ.

I wish when the Spirit of Christ silenced the "bad dog" within my flesh that I would have understood more clearly the tools in which He used to silence it. Being a "babe" in Christ, I was simply enjoying the presence of His Spirit. I did not realize it at the time that it was my relationship with Him through His Word that kept me filled with His Spirit and suppressed the "bad dog" within me. As life began to get busy, I slowly found myself not reading God's Word. The busier life got, the less time I found myself spending with Christ through His Word. I was busy serving the Church and I forgot who I was supposed to be serving. It was not long before the "bad dog" in my flesh began winning the battle. It began by winning small battles first, but it did not take long to see myself faced with large battles that I was also losing to the temptation of my flesh. I wanted to seek help, but the embarrassment that came with my personal battle always stood in the way.

My first mistake was waiting for my sinful actions to be exposed before seeking help. God's Word promises that a Christians sins will be exposed. **"But if ye will not do so, behold, ye have sinned against the Lord: and be sure your sin will find you out" (Numbers 32:23).** Yes, my sins were exposed and only then did I begin to get the help I had needed for years. Although I was finally getting help, I was not spared from the consequences of my actions. I found myself lying on my back inside the Vanderburgh County Jail. My sin brought forth a year sentence in jail, which brought great hardship to my family, church and friends. I felt like crawling in a hole and never coming out. The humiliation of my falling into this sin was much greater than it would have been to seek help when it began. To those reading this, I pray you will heed to the lessons I have learned so your journey in this life will not be hindered.

The one thing everyone in jail has working in their favor is time to think. The time to think can be a good thing if it is used to correct wrong thinking. That is what I chose to do with my time. I chose to evaluate where things went wrong in my life. When I examined my bad choices, I realized I made them because I was not reading scripture and applying its truths to my life on a daily basis. I allowed myself to get so busy serving in different ministries within the church that I forgot the true source of strength to accomplish those ministries. This strength comes through the Holy Spirit in reading the Word of God.

The main ministry that I was involved in was the bus ministry. I began this ministry with a passion to reach inner-city kids for Christ at a younger age than I was reached. But, through my neglecting to read God's Word and because I got caught up in the weekly competitions between the buses to see who could get the most kids, my real purpose for the ministry got lost. We had as many as 64 kids in one week, which to the best of my memory set a record. The competitions themselves were not a bad thing. They just made me feel like God was still using me despite my sin. In reality, the bus ministry had nothing to do with me. It was all about Christ and His love for those kids. When my sins were exposed, I lost the ministries I was serving within the Church. The bus ministry took the biggest hit. I am sure the news of my actions got out and although no one within the ministry was involved almost everyone stopped attending. That has been the hardest reality for me to live with even to this day. I will probably never know how many people my sins affected, but the lack of attendance sure gave me an idea of the impact.

While sitting in jail thinking of the impact my sins had on the ministries I once served, I knew I had to look forward not backwards. As bad as I felt about my past, I knew there was nothing I could do about it other than clean up my own life. My past was water under the bridge that could never be changed. It was around my third day in jail that I began speaking to the guys in my cell block about my experience with Christ. That night, I was given the opportunity to share my full testimony of how I accepted Christ. There were about 16 guys present all listening attentively. After sharing my experience in accepting Christ, I was approached by a man that wanted to accept Christ. I was blessed that night with the opportunity to witness this man accept Christ as his Savior. We stayed up half the night talking about the Lord. It was an awesome time of worship. It was just a few days after this night that the guards came and moved this guy from our cellblock. I could only assume that his time to be transported to Prison had come. I prayed and asked the Lord to be with him and to keep him in God's Word. Then the guards came and picked me up. I was moved to the Warrick County Jail. This was a Department of Correction holding facility where I would spend the remainder of my time in jail.

I began reading scripture again on a daily basis. It wasn't long before different inmates would stop by my night cell to ask questions about what I was reading. I recall being scared to answer questions about God's Word with other inmates. I felt inadequate and unworthy to open God's

Word with them. Every day while I was reading scripture, other inmates would find opportunities to ask questions. I would simply brush them off with a generic response to pacify them. I wanted to help them, but I felt the darkness of my past overshadowing the light of God's Word in my life. I was hesitant to represent Christ due to the fear of the other inmates finding out about my past, which would erase everything I had shared with them. I did not want my past to be used to hinder the cause of Christ in their lives, so I felt it best to keep silent. Then one night I was lying on my bunk when the Lord hit me with His scripture. **"Remember therefore from whence thou art fallen, and repent, and do the first works . . ." (Revelation 2:5).** I began thinking about those words, repent and do the first works. His scripture revealed to me that after my repentance I was obligated to continue my work for Him. The Holy Spirit through God's Word helped me understand that through His forgiveness I've been set free to serve Him once again.

It was around this time that I really could have used a visit from my pastor. I am sure he had plans to visit, but I really needed someone to talk to while the Lord was dealing with me. I didn't have the option to call him. His phone did not accept collect calls. During this time, I had the opportunity to speak with someone from Gideon's International. The Gideon's are a group of professional Christian men who wanted to share Christ with inmates in jail. I was excited. The Lord knew I needed to talk with someone. So, I signed up and went to hear what the Gideon's had to say. I had no idea who I was going to be speaking with, but in good faith I trusted the Lord would lead me to the right person. I ended up speaking with a man who owned an insurance company and who loved the Lord with all his heart. He was a great encouragement to me. We agreed to meet every Saturday morning and began to build a good relationship. I thought it was amazing how the Lord brought this man into my life. I was blesses by his willingness to encourage me through God's Word even though he had never met me before.

The good Lord began to open doors for me to share Him with those He wanted to reach. I was excited to be used by the Lord again. I thought I could never be used again. This is when I met another Christian that was in my cell block. He too was having the same issues with thinking he was unusable due to his past sins. I was able to share with him how God's Word spoke to me in Revelation 2:5. The Holy Spirit used this verse to speak to this young man as well. I was filled with much joy on that night seeing the Holy Spirit at work in someone else's heart. My love for Christ grew so much on that night. I just lay in bed and wept in joy. I knew at that moment that Christ still loved me, and He wanted to love others through me. My ministry to the Lord changed that night. It was no longer about what I could do for Christ. It became about what Christ could do for others through me.

Christmas was right around the corner and my Christian friend and I began to pray for a way we could share the love of Christ with our entire cell block. We decided to work with one another to build a Christmas tree from toilet paper and a commissary note pad. After constructing it, I remember watching the excitement in my friend's eyes as he used his color pencils to bring life to the tree. Then both he and I used the money our loved ones left on our books to buy gifts for every inmate in our cell block. We used our commissary note pad to wrap all of our gifts. We placed the name of each inmate on the gift designated for them. Then on Christmas Eve night, we stopped the night guard that walked by our night cells. We asked if he would mind placing the gifts under our make-shift Christmas tree. He was very pleased with our idea and was more than willing to help. We learned that night that he, too, was a Christian as he shared his faith with us.

The next morning when we woke up, a lot of the guys were already out in the day cell opening their gifts. No one ever said or asked anything, but I am sure they knew where the gifts came from. I do know some of them hadn't received a gift for a number of years. I learned that by simply listening to the guys while they were playing cards and or the board games we purchased for them. There is a true sense of freedom that comes from giving to others. This blessing can be received no matter where you are. Performing acts of kindness toward others brings about a freedom that no one can take from you, regardless of where you may be or what you did in your past.

My Christian friend and I began reading scripture and praying together. We would pray for opportunities for other inmates to hear God's Word. Those opportunities didn't take long to arrive. One at a time the men would stop by our cell and ask questions or share problems they were having. Before we knew it, we were sitting in our night cell with five other guys having a Bible study. We all decided to meet every other day after breakfast. This allowed us, on the day off, to prepare for each Bible study. The times my friend and I spent preparing for those Bible studies were times I will never forget. Those were some of my best times—spending time in God's Word. We would daily sharpen one another through the Word and lessons learned throughout each others' lives.

Although I was incarcerated and missed my family more than I could explain in words, I had a sense of peace within myself. I knew that the Lord was not done with me. I knew that there was still a purpose for me in this world, and all I had to do was seek Him daily with faith knowing He would direct my path. I knew then that my purpose was to help the men in my cell block grow in Christ. So, that is what I set out to do by sharing with them the many truths in scriptures. We met faithfully every other day to read God's Word. Each day was filled with different questions or problems the men had weighing on their hearts. We dealt with each situation one at a time. When we didn't know a precise answer, both my friend and I would be honest and say so. The men knew that neither of us was ordained ministers. They understood clearly that we were just forgiven sinners. This gave us the opportunity to share Christ with each one of the inmates.

As days turned to weeks and weeks into months, we watched each of the five men in our Bible study come to know Christ one at a time. There were two men in our cell block that would try to debate us on a daily basis. We would simply invite them to our Bible study. While we were having our study, they both would ritually pray every morning facing east. This is when I was introduced to the influence of the Muslim faith while incarcerated. As a group, we decided to move our study back to not compete with the prayer time set aside for these men. We wanted the door to be open for them to join our study time as well. This turned out to be a good call, because within a week, one of the Muslims joined our study time. He would just sit and listen without any questions, but showed the upmost respect for the Book we were reading. We all were really praying for him to be saved as well as the other Muslim that refused to be part of our study group. This young man would faithfully attend our studies in God's Word, while at the same time he would faithfully pray five times each day with his Muslim friend. This man's desire to seek after God was very impressive to me. He showed great commitment and faithfulness to his means of worship.

One afternoon he stopped by my night cell in tears torn with everything he had been learning. I shared with him that

God is not the author of confusion. I told him, "The Lord desires to fill your heart with His Spirit, which will bring you peace of mind and contentment within your soul."

He looked at me with tears flowing down his face. I felt the pain coming from his visible emotions. I was inwardly praying that the Lord would lead him to the point of salvation.

Then I asked him, "Would you like to receive the forgiveness the Lord longs to give you?" He said, "Yes". I explained to him that receiving Christ is more than praying a simple prayer. The Holy Spirit is what draws a person to accept Christ. If you mean this with all your heart then your spirit has already been regenerated. He understood, so together we kneeled to pray and I led him through a simple salvation prayer as he repeated what I said. It went something like this, "Lord I believe with all my heart that you died for my sins and rose from the dead three days later. Please forgive me for all I've done and fill me with your Spirit today. Today I give my heart and life to you Lord. Please receive me unto yourself. Thank you so much for saving me Jesus. In your name I pray—Amen!"

At that moment, I felt so free that there was nothing the State could do to take that sense of freedom away. That young man was the one that received Christ, but my heart was also filled with the love of Christ. Although I knew I was in jail being punished for sin that overtook my life, I knew that the Lord was using me and was more than able to continue using me for His purpose. I knew that for me to truly clean up my life I had to do more than just overcome my struggle with sin. I had to allow Christ to come alive in my heart for others. There is freedom that comes by being used by Christ when reaching out to others. This freedom can be experienced by anyone no matter what they may have done or where they may be. All that is required is a heart of repentance, Christ-like love toward others and a passion to serve the Lord.

Ch. 3

†

STRONG SUPPORT SYSTEM

The need for a strong support system is very important in being released from jail. There are many issues that can hit you when returning to society. Facing these issues all alone intensifies the impact of problems you will face. Having no support will greatly increase your chances of being incarcerated again. Everyone needs a place to call home, a place of employment to provide for that home, and someone to help with personal accountability to stabilize the home. Having family outside prepared to assist you in getting back on your feet is a huge blessing. If that's not possible, then find a local church to assist you. Depending on your location, there may even be government programs to help you through your parole office. It takes some humility to seek help after being released, but it is imperative if you want to increase your chance of freedom.

Roughly three months before my release, I was approached by my wife that she was being strong-armed by the Child Protective Service to divorce me. They told her that if she would simply divorce me our legal file would be closed. At that point, the only way it would be reopened was if there were any other accusations. Meaning, if we chose to be remarried after I was released, they could do nothing about it. This seemed like a reasonable solution, so I agreed to sign the paperwork as required. I did not realize it at the time, but signing those divorce papers, however good the intent, created a gulf between my wife and me. She began writing and visiting less often as the days turned to weeks until finally she stopped altogether. Then one night when I called her, she broke the news to me. She had met someone else. I will never forget when she said, "He's a nice guy, and under different circumstances you two would really like one another."

About one month later I received the legal papers telling me our divorce was final. I went to bed that night with a major headache. I learned firsthand that night how stress affects your health. I woke up the next morning with that same headache. I could not deal with the pain. Every sound around me was magnified and banging around in my head. It seemed like the guys in the day cell purposely got much louder once they learned what was going on with me. I was lying in my bed in tears dealing with both physical and emotional pain. I was aware that my testimony was being tested, but at the same time I wanted to crack the skull of the guys I felt were trying to get under my skin. I finally couldn't take it anymore. I walked up to the guard speaker box and requested to be put in solitary confinement for medical reasons.

I figured 24 hours alone would give me time to get my thoughts together. Little did I know that they would leave me in there for 72 hours! I found out later that 72 hours was the minimum solitary confinement schedule. Sitting in that small room with nothing to do for three days but to read and pray allowed for a lot of time to think. I just could not come to terms with the loss I was experiencing. It built up a lot of bitterness in my heart. I thought spending time in that cell would help me regroup, but it only hardened my heart by giving me time to imagine what my wife may be doing. Upon my release from solitary confinement, I was returned back to my cell block. In my absence, my Christian friend was moved. His turn to rotate just happened to come up while I was gone. The other men in my cell, who were also part of my Bible study, tried to console me. I appreciated their kind words, but my hardened heart was not soaking in a word they were saying. The men knew I was going through a rough time, so they chose to give me space.

About one month later, a letter from my lawyer came. I was getting out of jail early due to my sentence modification. Anyone else receiving such a letter would be excited, but I was too heartbroken. I had no idea what I was going to do. I lost my wife, my family, my home, my car, my job, everything except the suit I had on my back when I got sentenced in court almost a year earlier. I couldn't even attend church because my family was going there. This was about the scariest moment in my life. I seriously had no idea what I was going to do. Upon my release, my mother met me outside the jailhouse to take me to her house. I was in a complete daze knowing only that I had a place to sleep for awhile. I went out the next day trying to find work only to be turned down time after time. No one wanted to hire an ex-con regardless of the circumstances. I ended up settling with driving a cab from 7pm till 7am. It wasn't long until I realized driving a cab was not a good way to make a living.

As a cab driver, you are considered a contractor for which you are responsible to meet the nightly lease and to fill the tank up before returning the cab. Any money beyond that was considered profit. I would work the full twelve-hour night shift. Still I found myself owing the cab company money on the lease. It basically meant I worked the entire night for nothing. It didn't take long to see how the cab drivers were making side money by transporting drugs instead of passengers. This clearly wasn't anything I wanted to get involved in. There was no way I was going to take a risk on returning to jail. Then, the bills began to pile up including everything from probation fees to child support. It was obvious that I could not pay these mounting bills by simply driving a cab. Being on probation put me in a place where my fees had to be paid as did my child support. A failure to pay either one would land me in jail. This would place another level of pressure on me. It was becoming clear to me that I was heading to jail regardless of what I did considering I could not make enough money to pay my bills. If I chose to live as many of the other drivers, I took the risk of going to jail due to violating other laws.

I did not have much of a support system. Due to my divorce, I couldn't attend my old church because of the restraining order placed on me at the time of my release. I tried visiting other churches, but my heart was too hardened to hear truly what they were saying. I even visited my old church on occasions when my family was not there. I told them about my job situation. They encouraged me to find something else. I never told them of my financial crisis because I felt they had done enough for me. After all, they paid my mortgage the entire time I was incarcerated. I eventually stopped attending church altogether because of the reality that I couldn't attend my old church and the fact that my heart was hardened in bitterness over the entire situation. I decided to work the Sunday shift as well. My pride of wanting to figure this out on my own was not a good idea. It did not take long until I found myself in some pretty hairy situations. I didn't ask for these situations, but nevertheless they fell my way. Instead of doing the right thing, I gave in to my need for cash.

I found myself driving different clients around in the cab, picking up drugs to feed their addictions. I did not think I could be held accountable for what my passengers were doing, although I knew very well what they were up to. They would always tip me well for keeping my mouth shut during the whole ordeal. It didn't take long before my involvement got much deeper due to clients in my cab leaving unknown amounts of drugs under the back seat of my cab. All I was told is that I would eventually pick up a passenger that requested my cab number; they would retrieve it and I would get a nice tip. Everything I did was being done right there in the city cab while working. I found myself running drugs without even knowing either party. One party would stash it while the other party would pick it up. My only involvement was keeping my mouth shut and accepting their healthy tips.

I hated what I was doing, but I could not find another job to get out of the situation. I still was miserable both in how I was making a living and because I was alone. I would volunteer for all the cab fares no one wanted to pick because of the robberies that occurred in those locations. It seemed like I was on a suicide mission due to the emotional pain I was dealing with. I just wanted my sadness to end no matter how it took place. Deep in my soul I knew what I was doing was wrong, but between the bitterness in my heart and my inability to find another job, I found a way to justify my behavior. I still felt all alone during that time in my life. None of my past Christian friends were trying to reach me. This just intensified my bitterness at the time. I felt like they just wanted me to go away. But, it became clear to me that they were praying for me. When I would lie down at night all alone, I would feel the Holy Spirit attempting to draw me to repentance, but I would struggle every night to ignore Him.

Then one night while sitting in my apartment all alone, I was really troubled by the Holy Spirit. I knew I had to do something to get out of the situation I was in. So, I randomly opened the Bible to Proverbs and read, **"The fear of the Lord prolongeth days: but the years of the wicked shall be shortened" (Proverbs 10:27).** I fell to my knees asking the Lord to help me get out of the situation I was in. It has been so easy to blame my sins on the people who hurt me as a child. I knew that everything I had done and have been doing was generated from my own wicked heart. I needed to repent and make things right again with the Lord, so that is exactly what I sought out to do.

I felt before I could truly get things right with the Lord that I needed to ask forgiveness of my family for the consequences I had brought on them. I had received their forgiveness for the wrong I had done in the past, but that was well before the consequences took effect. I wasn't having any contact with my ex-wife at the time. I truly didn't think she would listen to me considering everything I put her through. In desperation, I asked my mom to write her a note. I knew they were always close and figured it was worth a shot. In that note, I enclosed a CD that I had worked on for hours. It was full of our favorite love songs. I was hoping that she would be drawn back to the days when those songs meant something to her. I cried the whole time I made it, praying the Lord would give me another chance to make things right in my life. I realized during that prayer that Jesus truly understood my pain because He, on several occasions through the Holy Spirit, brought back the love songs from His Word to my memory, hoping they would draw me back to the days when they meant something to me. I fell to my knees in tears crying to the Lord the truths of His Word, **"For a just man falleth seven times, and riseth up again: but the wicked shall fall into mischief" (Proverbs 24:16).** I knew with all of my heart that the day I accepted Christ I was truly remorseful of my sins and through that remorse I asked Christ to forgive my sins. My trust was placed solely on Him that day for salvation. I knew that through Him I was made a just man. I also knew that I had fallen into sin a number of times. I prayed unto the Lord asking Him to forgive me of all my transgressions and to raise me up to the place where He could use me again.

I truly wanted to get things right in my life. I mailed the CD and the note my mom wrote hoping it would lead to some form of communication between us again. I waited for days for a response thinking she threw the entire package away. Then, I got a call. It was her! I was so excited I could hardly breathe. She was so glad to receive my mom's note along with the CD of our favorite songs. I was like a teenage boy on the phone with his first girlfriend. I was so grateful for the opportunity to hear her sweet voice again. All she agreed to was a date and then we would see what happened. I dropped to my knees asking the Lord to help me be the man she deserved. I wanted with all my heart to become the man my family needed. I knew right then I had to find some help. I needed a support system—something I should have sought upon my release from jail.

I met with the pastor of my old church to express my desire to get my life back on track. He said the hardest step had just been made by coming to him for support. He told me the next thing I needed to do was come back to church. By this time the restraining order had been lifted, so I did not have any legal restraints. Talk about awkward! I had been away from church for well over a year. My ex-wife and three children still attended there, so you would think it would be easy to go back. But, I was fearful people would look down on me for my past. I knew I needed the people of God to bring me closer to Christ, so I went back that following Sunday.

Yes, some people looked down on me. Some even purposely avoided me. I did feel completely out of place around those people; although I wasn't surprised by the response I received from them. I'm sure they were frightened of me considering that I had betrayed their trust. Thankfully, there were plenty of other Christians that were very glad to see me. They said they have been praying diligently for my entire family. I thanked them from the bottom of my heart and asked for continued prayer. I shared with them how their prayers had spared me from a lot of problems. I truly believe that those prayers were what kept God's loving hands of grace on me especially during the times I rightfully deserved to be thrown right back in jail. It took me almost two years after my release to discover my need for a solid support system. The local church was developed by the Lord himself for this very reason.

After my release from jail, the Court ordered me to participate in counseling through the Southwestern Indiana Mental Health Center (SWIMHC). As I was going through the sessions I pre-judged the outcome, expecting that I wouldn't get anything out of it. I felt that the counseling I was receiving in God's Word was more than sufficient in bringing about my total recovery. I learned, though, that God was involved with the intimate details of my life. He had used both forms of counseling I was receiving to mold me into His image. The therapy I had received at SWIMHC helped me to look at the consequences I had brought to my victim. That was easy for me to comprehend, since, I, too, was a victim of sexual abuse; although, up to this point in my therapy, I didn't understand the level of impact the abuse had on my thinking process. This really helped me to understand the impact of the choices I had previously made. I came to understand that the influences in my childhood were deeply engrained in my thought process. Both means of the counseling was used to redirect my thinking pattern. They both pointed out the reality of how selfish sexual abuse is. They both highlighted the importance of thinking of others and the consequences created by my actions. They also both emphasized the need for accountability; they just had different methods of providing it.

I was disappointed that, during our group sessions, my therapist wouldn't allow me to share with the group the many lessons I was learning through my biblical counseling at church. He would stop me each time in subtle yet obvious ways. I didn't let that stop me, though. I continued bringing up biblical principles if I thought it applied to the subject matter we were dealing with. I came to the conclusion that both forms of counseling were exactly what I needed. Also through my biblical counseling I learned that regardless of the influences of my past, it was my sinful, wicked heart that drew me to feed upon my lust. In gaining understanding of my sinful nature, it enabled me to come to terms with the sinful nature of "my" abusers/victimizers as well. This recognition helped me to properly forgive them, knowing these individuals needed help with their own sinful nature, just as I did. I came to the realization that both forms of counseling had served me well. I became well balanced in my understanding of the changes I needed to make—both mentally and spiritually. These changes ranged from changing my patterns of behavior to how I viewed the way I was worshipping Christ each day. The most important concept that I had received was the knowledge that I wasn't alone. I had plenty of people from all different spectrums in life that wanted to see me succeed.

The encouragement that I had received from those I knew and loved was the most helpful, though. The burden that they had for my entire family showed through their actions. The fact that my life was being pieced back together proved to me the importance of a strong support system. It wasn't just me growing stronger—it was my entire family. We were all growing closer to one another as well. Our focus was on loving God and others—not loving ourselves above everyone else. I was also encouraged not to allow my past to hold me back in seeking other employment. This encouragement eventually opened the door for a different job at a local window factory. This helped me to meet my financial obligations.

It was during the early stages of this time period that my ex-wife Donna decided to leave the other guy she had met. I was so excited. This guy had it all: his own business, a nice sports car, a customized van, and a motorcycle. All I had was a repentant heart and the desire to be used by God. I was so humbled by the love that both the Lord and Donna showed me. I wanted with all of my heart to repay their love with a life committed to serving God. So, I began to faithfully attend church and began serving the Lord through my church in different ways. My heart's desire was for the Lord to develop a ministry within the church that would help hold one another accountable. This burden was derived from His Word, **"Exhort one another daily, while it is called today; lest any of you be hardened through the deceitfulness of sin" (Hebrews 3:13).** I did not want the way I had previously slipped into sin and had my heart hardened to the Word of God to be in vain. I wanted to do all I could to stop that from happening to anyone else. I knew in my heart that my past could be used for the good of others.

About a month later on Valentine's Day of the year 1998, I leased a limo for a glamorous date with Donna. I picked her up with the excitement of a teenager picking up his first date for the prom. She looked as beautiful as the first day I met her. As we enjoyed our ride around the city, I knelt down on one knee to ask the biggest question of my life. I dazed into her gorgeous eyes and asked, "Will you give me the honor and marry me again? I promise to be the husband that you have always deserved." Her eyes began to flood in tears as she said, "Yes, I would love to be your wife again." This was an amazing moment for me that I actually had an opportunity to propose to my wife. The first time we were married that decision was brought on by our salvation and realization that we were living in sin. Now, we both just sat there holding one another in tears thanking the Lord for everything he had brought us through.

At last, my life was coming back together. I could not refrain from hugging my soon to be bride and crying in joy. I knew at that point I was being given that second chance that I had prayed for with all my heart. The good Lord had revealed Himself to me once again, showing me the power of His grace through this second chance. We decided to get remarried on our tenth year anniversary of the day we met—August, 19th of 1998. Our engagement lasted only a few months, but it felt like years. Considering our divorce was a private matter, we chose to make our second wedding a private matter as well. We decided to invite close family members to our wedding, which was the most beautiful day in my family's life. I do not think there was a dry eye in the service. The testimony of reunification and the power of forgiveness were overwhelming to everyone involved. Having my family back together again gave me a solid support system. I still thank God everyday for bringing my family back together.

Ch. 4

†

A FRACTURED FAMILY

The consequence of such an event on a family has long lasting effects many of which were experienced by my family. My wicked heart brought on much anguish to my family. This anguish was handled directly by my wife, Donna; therefore, I thought it would be best for her to tell you her side of the story. I hope that hearing how such an act affects families will play a part in stopping this from destroying other families.

As a wife, I experienced a lot of emotions through this ordeal. My heart was broken. My trust was shattered and my faith was tested all at the same time. I had to find a way to continue raising three young children all by myself. When my husband's sinful behavior was exposed, I, like most women wanted to pack up and leave. I was both saddened and angered all at the same time. Beyond all else, I wanted to make sure that my children were in a safe environment. In knowing firsthand the details of my husbands' past behavior, I chose to press forward with trying to forgive. Dennis and I began counseling immediately with our pastor, where we worked to reconcile our fractured family.

After about two months into our counseling, a couple that we were really close to decided to leave the church for various reasons. They played a pivotal role in our getting grounded with our faith in Christ. They took us under their wings to disciple us through God's Word in an intimate way. They were well aware of our situation and convinced us to move with them thinking we would be better served at the other church they planned to attend. The pastor there was very intelligent in the Word of God, as is the pastor at our home church. The people of that church were as sweet as could be. Everyone was very loving. Not one person passed judgment one way or another on my family. That was very important for us to be able to grow as we so desperately needed. Then, after a few months of attending this new church, Dennis and I started realizing that they were very strict. When we met with one of the deacons and the pastor about joining the church, a bomb was dropped in our lap.

The leadership at the church felt it would be best if we separated ourselves from our extended family. They did not want us to have anything to do with our parents, our siblings, or other loved ones. They figured that our past would be better left behind us. They told us that as members we would have to submit to the leadership of the church. They quoted scripture to support their request, **"Obey them that have the rule over you, and submit yourselves: for they watch for your souls, as they that must give account, that they may do it with joy, and not with grief: for that is unprofitable for you" (Hebrews 13:17).** The pastor even came to the meeting with a check in hand to assist us in paying to get our phone numbers changed. All we had to do was agree not to give the number out to any of our family members. This entire request was baffling to both me and Dennis. We knew that we needed time to think about this request.

We went ahead and changed our phone number as requested by the church leadership; plus, we kept our distance from our family as requested. Doing this did not seem right. How were we to reach our family for Christ living like this? It simply made no sense. How was this in line with God's Word? I called my mother about this request made by the church leadership. She understandably was concerned with the direction our family was heading. I told her we did not feel right about this course of action and we were going to do something about it. Dennis decided to return the check for the phone bill they offered us, along with a note. The note stated, "We agree whole heartedly with the scripture you read in Hebrews that we need to submit to the church leadership the Lord has placed us under. That is why we must return to our home church where we were saved to submit to their leadership."

Meanwhile, my mother was highly concerned with the church we were attending because they wanted to isolate us from our family. She took matters into her own hands and decided to report the past actions of my husband to the proper authorities. I am sure she was concerned that our entire family was being place in a vulnerable situation by staying at that church. She clearly took this course of action well before I had a chance to tell her we left that church. I didn't even know that she had called the authorities until they showed up to bring my husband in for questioning. I sat at home in the dark not knowing what was going to happen to my family. I just sat and prayed for the Lord to intervene in some way to keep our family together.

After what seemed to be several hours, Dennis called stating he thought it would be best to be honest. He told me he formally acknowledged his wrongs and was willing to pay whatever debt he owed to society. Then he told me he had to move out of the home while he started his legal proceedings. I started crying. Why was this happening? Everything was going so good. Our family was already healing from the past. Dennis comforted me by reminding me of the sovereignty of Christ. We have to trust that everything will be alright at the end of this journey. At that time, neither he nor I had a clue as to how long that journey was going to be.

It wasn't long before I received a letter in the mail from our local Courts Division. They wanted me to appear in Family Court. I was really at a loss with this request. I thought, "What have I done?" Dennis received notification from the courts around the same time concerning his sentencing date. I was in contact with him every chance I could get. Both I and the children really missed him. When going to my court date, I learned that this was going to be a weekly event. The courts wanted to make sure that the kids remained in a safe environment. After the events that occurred in my family, I could understand their concerns.

Within weeks of my court date, Dennis had to appear in court to be sentenced. We met with his attorney before having to appear in court to go over the events about to take place. He and I were really concerned when leaving the attorney's office. We both realized that even though we were broke, our car was nicer then the car driven by Dennis' attorney. How could our car be better than that of his attorney? I still remember us pulling behind the attorney's car to follow him to court. Dennis stated, "Look at his car; I'm going to jail!" Anyone else in that position may have laughed, but neither of us was in a laughing mood. We were just trusting God knowing that the law firm we hired was recommended to us by our pastor.

Dennis chose to take a plea deal which left the option of sentencing solely up to the judge. This was his decision trusting that the Lord would direct the judge as He saw fit. He thought it was important to place his fate in God's hands which turned out to be reasonable. Dennis' sentence was three years and six months with one year and six months of that sentence to be served on probation. They also ordered him to register on the Indiana Sex Offender Registry for 10 years. My husband took a brief look back as the deputy led him off to jail. I wanted so much to run up there to embrace him one last time. I noticed he whispered, "I love you!" I just stood there in tears, whispering the same words right back to him.

Life without my husband wasn't easy. I had to face the reality that the family courts wanted me to divorce him. Every week they would continually slam me with remarks trying to encourage me to leave him. "Why are you still married to this man?" "You really need to move on with your life, and do what is best for your kids." Then they would question my judgment which brought them to question my parental ability. They continued this pattern week after week, I would simply say, "My husband has been through a lot in his life just as I have. He is not the person you are making him out to be. I believe in forgiveness and have given that forgiveness to my husband." That did not persuade them at all. They were determined to see us divorced.

I listened to this for months, holding off their continued bashing of my husband. Then, a case worker approached me after court to tell me, "If you would just divorce your husband we could close your case file and you would not have to come back here anymore. Then, after your husband gets out and if you so choose to get remarried, there is nothing we could do because your file will be closed." That option seemed so enticing. I felt it would lighten my load so much. The following week, I chose to tell the judge that I wanted to know what I needed to do to file for divorce. They were more than willing to give me all the direction I needed. They pointed me to the Legal Aid Society for support. I learned there that when your spouse is incarcerated, you can actually file for a divorce and it will only cost one dollar. I then had the heart breaking responsibility to share this with Dennis. I tried to explain the details to him, but I knew no matter what I said it would break his heart. I felt I at least owed him an explanation, so when he called I shared with him the best I could.

It wasn't easy explaining to the children where their daddy was every day. They were simply too young to understand what was going on, but I was honest with them anyway. We went through so much hardship during this time. I leaned on my mother a lot for support. My family and I still went to church every chance we could. My church was a huge help financially. They offered to pay our monthly mortgage while Dennis was in jail. There were different members of the church that would ask me how I was doing when they bumped into me at church. But, outside of church I did not hear from anyone. I did get a lot out of God's Word during the services, but I really could have used extra support outside of Sunday.

I admit I did not read God's Word like I should have but I did pray often. I sensed the Holy Spirit with me during these hard times. The good Lord provided the grace needed for me to get by each day. I simply had a hard time applying His grace to the emotions I was dealing with. There was a part of me that gradually grew cold against my husband. The pain that our family was enduring was due to the choices he had made; therefore, in reality it was his fault we were going through all this. I was even being advised by different members of my church to sever ties with Dennis and move on. It was not long before I lost the emotional attachment to him. My feelings for him at that time would be better described as "disappointing". I had lost the unchanging love that I thought would never go away. Then, the final divorce papers came in the mail. I seriously felt free of the entire burden I had been carrying for so long.

I had a brigade of people encouraging me to move on with my life and no one encouraging me to hold on. After months of hearing, "You need to move on", I came to terms with that reality; so, that is what I sought out to do. I placed my personal information on the local dating line to see what would happen. Sure enough, I got bombarded with calls many of which were questionable. I did find one guy on there that sparked my interest. He seemed like he had his life together financially. I agreed to a date after a lengthy phone conversation. He was a nice guy and treated me like a lady. He never made any inappropriate advances toward me to make me feel uncomfortable; so, I agreed to go on other dates with him. To be straight forward, it helped me forget about the emotional pain I had been experiencing during that year.

It wasn't long after the divorce was finalized that my now "ex-husband" was released from jail. I didn't want to have anything to do with him. I knew his smooth words would melt my heart. I wasn't going to have it. I needed to move on. This belief was magnified when I learned that Dennis was posted all over the internet as a registered sex offender. Talk about embarrassing! I wanted to pack up everything and move my kids to another state. Trying to comfort my kids when they were harassed by other kids who knew their dad was on the internet was very difficult. It was so unfair to the kids. The kids were too young to understand this ordeal. All they knew was that they loved their daddy. I knew the kids harassing them were too young to understand the extent of what was going on. This told me that their parents were playing a big role in what they knew. It was not hard to figure that out when their parents could not even look me in the eyes. I just wanted to yell at them, "What did me or my children do to you?" How could they treat us this way when they knew I had divorced their dad? I realize the parents did not know the details of my husband's situation leaving them to think the worst. I am sure they did not mean any harm to my children, but never the less my children experienced the backlash just the same. I really loved Dennis, but the repercussions of what he did were too great for me to deal with.

Although I was occasionally dating the guy I met on the local date line, this time was the loneliest point in my life. I knew deep in my heart that I needed to get things right with the Lord. When I would pray to ask the Lord for help in times of trouble, I would think of my ex-husband. I knew he wanted to make things work between us, and I knew he was terribly hurt because of the pain he had placed us in. I had already forgiven him for his past actions, but now I knew I needed to forgive him for the consequences we had been enduring because of those actions. Then, I received a letter in the mail from my ex-husbands mom along with a recorded CD filled with a lot of my favorite love songs. I really missed her. She was like a mom to me in so many ways. I know she only wanted what was best for us all. I quickly learned through the note how much Dennis missed us all. To be truthful, we missed him too. I decided to call the number provided in the note to thank his mom and to set up a time for her to see the children. Thankfully, Dennis was there as well. I agreed to meet with him for a date at the Fall Festival. We had a great time together, as we have always had in the past.

To this day I still have that note, so I've decided to share it with you. It's was a pivotal moment in our relationship making it worthy of being in this book.

Donna,

Just writing to inform you that I'll grant you what you desire, by leaving you alone about the situation between you and Dennis. Although, I pray you will take a second to read this note. I do hope you both are able to work things out, I know you still love one another.

Dennis received his copy of the restraining order; he plans to follow it to the letter. He doesn't want to take any chances of going back to jail. So, you need not worry about him contacting you. His only desire is to remain good friends with you while maintaining a good relationship with both of your kids. I'm glad to hear through Dennis that you too wish to be friends. Who knows what can grow from a good friendship?

I can see how this temporary restraining order can cause you to avoid Dennis whenever possible. But, if you want to see him you can anytime and anywhere. Whether it is home alone or around others in public, I'm sure he will take what he can get. According to the restraining order as I read it, you all are allowed to have visitation together at anytime and anywhere you want with the kids. This means you all could go to the Fall Festival together or anywhere else you wish. Dennis has mentioned a great interest in taking you all to this year's Fall Festival. He knows you all have had some good times there in the past.

Everyone can tell by the expression on his face that he misses you all a great deal. I've spoken with him and he understands your need of space for time to heal from all he has put you through. If you wish to contact him feel free to use my number, I will be sure he gets the message.

I do ask as his mother, that you please cheer him up from time to time with a phone call. Visiting the kids with you there really makes his week. I hate seeing him so down, regardless of the reasoning. So, please call him soon.

Enclosed is a CD of songs that Dennis put together with you heavy on his heart. I hope that it touches you as it did Dennis when he put it together. He really loves you Donna and I have no doubt that he is truly sorry for everything he has put your family through. I know you've forgiven him for everything already, but that was well before all the consequences you've had to endure. Dennis is working diligently *to save money so he can meet any need you or the kids may have, so don't hesitate to seek his assistance if you need anything.*

Well, I'm going to let you go for now. I'll give you a call in a few days so I can visit my grandkids. I love you Donna and please let the kids know that their grandma loves them very much.

Love,
Linda Lou

Between receiving this note and listening to our favorite love songs, it made me really think about our family. I wanted to see if we could make things work. I was glad I decided to go on that date with Dennis. He looked so handsome and he treated me like gold the whole time we were together. We dated several times; each date became better than the last. I was falling in love with him all over again. I missed him so much. The kids were so glad to be able to spend time together again as a family. I loved the way the kids lit up around their daddy. I couldn't help but to imagine life together again.

It was around this time on Valentine's Day that he pulled up in a limo. He was so sweet. I could see how nervous he was when he got down on one knee to ask me to marry him. I was so excited. We really did not have a proper proposal before our first marriage. It was not long until we were re-married and working diligently to rebuild our family. Things were a lot better in every aspect of our lives. We were a family again doing everything that a normal family would do. Dennis was working at a window factory doing his best to provide for us. The kids were all in school happier then I had seen them in years. Everything was going great, and I was glad things were normal again—well, as close to normal as we could get anyway. Things were not perfect. Dennis couldn't move up at his place of employment. Unfortunately, having this black ball over his head overshadowed his ability to lead. Regardless of his work ethics and job performance, he would continue to be passed by when promotional opportunities would come up. This really placed us in a financial pinch, but the Lord always provided.

Due to repeated sexual offenses around the country by sex offenders, the media decided to promote the offenders website. By this time the kids were quite a bit older and were faced with the embarrassment of having a dad on this web site. We tried our best to prepare them over the years, knowing one day this would happen. Our daughter was confronted with the website when spending the night with a friend. They were surfing the web when her friend chose to search their neighborhood for sex offenders. Then she asked our daughter, "What is your address?" Our daughter was well aware of what she would find, but also knew her friend had a general idea of where she lived. So, she chose to be honest and tell the girl the address. Sure enough, she saw a picture of Dennis. Our daughter quickly explained that this was a long time ago and that her dad is one day going to be taken off the website. Dennis would always tell the kids that one day he would be removed from the website, even though he knew that the new laws set in place required him to report for life. He would always do his best to comfort us all when faced with the embarrassment of his past. I could tell in his eyes that he was saddened by how his past was still affecting us. I assured him that we loved him for who he was and that we had forgiven his past.

I really felt sorry for my husband. It was clear that society had permanently black balled him by requiring him to be on the Sex Offender Registry for life. I could tell he had lost his motivation which was unlike him. My husband has always been a self motivator. The reality of not even being able to crack the glass ceiling over his head was weighing him down. He would never admit it to me, but I knew he was concerned how this would affect our financial future. He always said that everything would work out fine. We just had to trust the Lord.

I can say that through this entire ordeal the good Lord had always met the needs of our family. He used the love of our local church to pay our mortgage. There is no doubt the house would have been lost without their help. He brought a kind family to our neighborhood with kids that were the same age as ours. This brought good companionship to our children and a good friend to me in their mother. There were many times when we would have monetary needs and the neighbors would offer to help out. The Lord knew what we needed and He brought it to us. We needed the outward showing of love of others, and the Lord brought that to us in several ways. Every time a need arose that I did not know how I was going to handle, the Lord would meet the need. Those needs were usually met through my neighbors who to the best of my knowledge were not Christians. The Lord did open the door for their children to attend church with me, and over time I was blessed to witness that they accepted Christ as their savior. These experiences made my faith in the Lord grow stronger. It made it much easier in trusting the Lord that everything would work out fine.

Ch. 5

†

THE GLASS CEILING

The glass ceiling is a barrier that prevents individuals from rising to positions of responsibility and economic security. It is most commonly used to explain discrimination issues in the work place. The effects of "The Glass Ceiling" are applicable to what I have experienced upon my release from incarceration. It is important to realize the consequences of having a felony hanging over your head. Having a felony, regardless of its title, creates a glass ceiling over your head that will prevent you from finding employment, or moving up at the place of employment that you may have found. Having the black ball of being registered as a sex offender only thickens that glass, making it impossible to break. Companies today are service oriented. This makes the need for them to update hiring practices a must to meet the concerns of society. This clearly affects the decision process when considering hiring a registered sex offender.

Upon my release, I could not find any form of employment. Everywhere I went simply turned me away or accepted my application with no intent of calling me back.

I had to make some sort of living, so I began driving a taxi cab, and at the time I thought it was the only thing I could do to survive. Thankfully, the Holy Spirit was encouraging me to straighten out my life. Despite my action, the Lord was not done with me. His Spirit impressed upon me every day, attempting to draw me back into His grace. My heart was broken by the unconditional love given to me as the Holy Spirit led me to repentance.

Not long after getting things right with the Lord, I heard of a position that was opening up at a local window factory. I was hesitant about sharing my past with any potential employer. It was simply embarrassing, but I was more nervous about being locked up again. I knew I had to get things right in my life. I chose to take the risk of being humiliated by applying for another job. At the point of being interviewed, I recognized the general manager. He was a local pastor that I had fellowshipped with when I was first saved. He knew my pastor. During the interview, the general manager was in the room as well. He asked me, "Have you placed your past behind you to the point that you are looking toward the future?" I said, "Yes!" However, that was not the complete truth. It is kind of hard placing your past behind you when it is like a black ball chained to your ankle preventing you from moving forward. He said they would give me a chance and placed me in the Woods Jam Department constructing windows for new homes.

This was my first real job since being released, and I was really excited. Since I was no longer driving a cab, I stopped my drug transporting immediately. I really wanted to get my life right, and this job was a good start. I worked hard every day committing myself to learning every aspect of the department. I went in to work one morning and the ball dropped on the entire department. The supervisor got fired, then the team lead builder quit, along with the other guys in the department. I was literally standing in the department all alone, knowing I needed my job. The guys that left attempted to get me to quit, but that was not an option for me.

The general manager approached me and asked me what I thought had happened. I told him there was a tight alliance with the supervisor, but that I was not a part of it. I told him I was capable of stepping up to any role he saw fit. The next day he took me up on that offer by asking me to keep building the ordered windows. There were a few new employees starting that day, and he needed me to step up and train each one of them. I saw this as an opportunity to prove my leadership ability, so I not only trained all the new hires, I did so by utilizing them to construct all the windows ordered each day without requesting any overtime. I led this team for about four months on my own doing so with great effectiveness. I really felt like I found a place I could build a career. Maybe I could eventually work my way to the role of supervisor a position I was already filling.

I was then hit with some bad news. I was introduced to my new supervisor at work. They decided to promote an attractive female employee from another department with no experience in my department at all. I was completely set aside by this news, so I met with the production manager. He said the company saw this as the best move at the time. He really appreciated all my hard work and stated he wanted me to show that same level of commitment by assisting the new supervisor. I clearly needed the job, so I moved forward with doing my job as instructed.

It was not long before I realized that I was still being utilized to supervise the department. I just was not getting the pay or title to do so. I worked diligently to train the new supervisor, but her lack of knowledge and experience was a huge hindrance. I then met with her and told her I was no longer going to be doing anything under her responsibility. I explained to her that I needed to focus on my position in order to meet the company's expectations. It was not long before we all began to work overtime on a daily basis. I liked the overtime, but I knew Management was eventually going to come down on us all for the issues going on in the department. I knew I had to jump ship, so I began to look for another job.

I made contact with my old friend with the Gideon's that visited me every Saturday while I was incarcerated. He was a strong encouragement to me, directing me through God's Word as I knew he would. He strongly encouraged me to volunteer with him in the prison ministry. There was a small group going to Wabash Correctional Facility and he really wanted me to attend these services. I was terrified, but I was also overwhelmed with the moving of the Holy Spirit to participate. I signed up with a great deal of nervousness.

As I was walking through the yard to the chapel at the Wabash Valley Correctional Facility, a man quickly ran up to me. He caught me completely by surprise, but it took only a second to realize who he was. He was the same man I witnessed accepting Christ a few years ago in the Vanderburgh County Jail. Through this reunion and the lessons during the chapel service, the Lord really revealed Himself to me. He showed me that He could still use me inside the prisons even though I was now on the outside. The Lord topped off this blessed day during our lunch break. I had met another volunteer that just happened to be part owner of the largest plumbing services in the tri-state. I was sharing my prayer request for new employment to the other men during lunch when he introduced himself. He told me that they were looking for a new warehouse manager, but he had to speak with the other two owners before he could offer me the position.

The opportunity filled my heart with excitement! My heart was filled with faith that everything was going to fall into place. That following Monday, I received a phone call. It was the gentleman I met at Wabash Valley Correctional Facility. He wanted me to come in for an interview to meet the other owners. I was excited for the opportunity, so I utilized a personal day to take that interview. I spoke to the owners about my desire to excel in the plumbing field. I told them I would like to one day be a union plumber. They hired me on the spot as warehouse manager. I was ecstatic!

I worked diligently for this company being responsible for prefabricating their tub and shower valves, pre-pulling the job orders for all the service trucks and keeping inventory on hand. I even learned how to turn tubs into whirlpools. Every time an opening would arise for an apprentice with the plumbers union, I would voice my interest. Every time I would be turned down, with the boss telling me I was doing such a great job in the warehouse. He would say that they needed me to stay where I was most effective. I would tell him that I needed to go where I could best provide for my family.

I requested to go out in the field with the plumbers, when time allowed, so I could learn the inventory I was managing. This opportunity got me out in the field where at least I could learn the trade. As I learned the inventory, I then began praying for an opportunity to move into the show room to help sell the inventory. Once again, every time an opening would arise, I would voice my interest in the position; however, as always I would get shot down with the same old line. I was content with where the Lord had me. I just did not want that contentment to make me comfortable. I have always been taught that getting comfortable in anything hinders how God can use you; so, I continued knocking on doors to see if the Lord would open something up. During my time working with this plumbing company, I learned a lot. The good Lord allowed me to use what I have learned to help with many plumbing projects at my church. He also allowed me to use my knowledge to provide me with a source of income by doing side jobs for family and friends.

I also worked hard to grow spiritually while working at this place. I met with a deacon at my church weekly for discipleship lessons. I opened up to him about a lot in my life sharing with him my past and how it has affected my life. We would pray for various issues going on in my life as I would share them. Having that one on one time with someone who is grounded in God's Word was important. It developed a friendship that was critical in my spiritual growth. Having someone to lean on with prayer requests and spiritual questions is important. The relationship that it creates is a perfect visual of the relationship that can be developed in Christ by spending time with Him in His Word.

I learned that viewing my service to my employer as simply serving my company was not thinking outside the box. It is important to realize that our level of service toward our employer is an act of obedience toward our Lord and Savior Jesus Christ. As Christians, we are serving a higher power than that of the power placed in charge of the company where we work. Everything we do should be done with all of our ability, performing each task with the level of ability required to please Christ. This is accomplished by having a Christ-like attitude. In order to maintain this spirit throughout the day, it must be purposed in our heart before each day begins. As we all know, there are many challenges that can test an individual throughout the day. In order to prepare to handle these challenges correctly, your heart must be purposed to do so in advance. The best way to be assured that you start the day out right is to do so in God's Word and in prayer.

I learned that the Lord uses the circumstances around you to lead you to His will. It was clear to me that I was not going to be able to move up in the company where I was working. I began to pray for another door to open, but I had no idea what that would be. A few months later, while in church, I heard that our part-time youth pastor was going to come on full-time. He was excited that he was going to be able to leave his position at his place of employment. I knew he worked for the deacon friend of mine as a warehouse associate. Maybe this was the door of opportunity that I had been praying for? I began focusing my prayers on this opening hoping the Lord would lay everything out for me to get the job.

After a few weeks of prayer and much thought, I approached my deacon friend. He immediately said, "I think you would be a perfect fit for the warehouse". The following

Monday, I received a call from the company. They wanted me to come in for an interview. I was hired instantly to oversee the flow of all the material in their warehouse. It was not a management position, but it started off $6,000.00 more annually than the management position I was leaving. The opportunity for growth in this telecommunication company was astounding. I knew I was way outside my comfort zone, but this is exactly what I was looking for. It not only provided for my family. It also provided a new sense of hope that one day I would be able to advance in my position.

By law, I was obligated to tell my employer about my felony which I had already done years before I was hired. Remember, my deacon friend helped me get this job. This was possible since he is the President of the company. He knew everything about me and hired me anyway. It is awesome how the church links every realm of society together. The most amazing thing is that when the church is Christ centered, all classes of society within that church are on the same level. The fact is that we are all sinners and in need of a savior. This unites us all together under Christ equally forgiven of our sins. The ground is level at the foot of the cross where sinners find themselves seeking the Lord. This truth is what kept my deacon friend from casting stones at me. He knows Christ is able to heal those struck by the sickness of sin. He did not approve of my past actions, and I am sure they turned his stomach, but, he forgave me. When giving me the opportunity to work for his company, he thought it best to keep my past between him and myself.

I felt completely humbled that this man was taking such a risk for me. I remember asking him, "What if someone notices my information on the sex offender's website?" He said he would deal with that if or when that happened. I was really hoping that would not happen. He did not see it as an issue either way considering I was working all alone in a warehouse. It did not take long though before someone discovered my information on line. After all, the company owned the local internet provider. Needless to say, the gossip started flying. The president decided to bring the issue up in his next management meeting. At this meeting, he told everyone that he was aware of my entire situation and had known me for a number of years. He told them he expected them to put a halt to the gossip within each of their departments. The fact that he was president and his judgment has always been trusted helped me a lot. I felt blessed having him in my corner. Gods grace in my life was exposed through this man's actions.

I clearly had to deal with the internal gossip and stares during company meetings. It was something I was already accustomed to. I was determined to prove myself worthy to have been hired. I wanted everyone in the company to see that the president made the right choice by hiring me. I wanted them to see that he did know the full extent of my situation and that is why he chose to take the risk with me. To me, that meant I had to learn every aspect of the department, and be able to run it effectively on a daily basis. I worked diligently to do just that and along the way I earned the trust of many associates that dealt with the warehouse.

I desired to move up in the company in order to better provide for my family. During this period, I was working with my second manager. She had been with the company for a number of years, but had never been over the warehouse. She placed a lot of trust in me. I feel I met this trust to the fullest extent of my knowledge. The company then hired a couple of other associates to assist in the warehouse due to the growth we were experiencing. This is when my manager decided to provide me with supervisor training. I was off work for two days at a seminar to learn different techniques to motivate and direct potential subordinates. I was excited. I saw this as a sign that I had a chance to advance.

Then out of nowhere my manager quit for unknown reasons and it was like the training I took left with her. My new manager was the father-in-law of another deacon in my church. I thought that would give us common ground to stand on and help me continue personal growth with the company. That clearly was not the case. Not long after he was hired, I was introduced to my new supervisor. He was hired from outside the company. Apparently he had previously worked in telecommunication with one of our engineers.

I was obviously upset, but I also knew my options were limited. I decided to make the best of the situation by helping the new supervisor learn the ropes. My intentions were to teach him everything I was doing, so he could take a lot of the pressure off me. After about three months, I realized that was not going to happen. I was still doing the supervisor position. I just was not the guy standing over everyone's shoulder acting like I knew what I was doing. I decided to meet with the warehouse manager to point out the obvious. It was not long until the company let him go. He clearly was not working out. One would think that they would consider me to fill this position, with all the responsibilities I had on my shoulders. But, the manager said the company decided there was no need for a supervisor at that point. It was clear to me that the glass ceiling over my head was affecting any opportunity for me to advance.

I was at the end of my rope. I could not understand why I was being treated in such a way. I began to pray, not for my advancement in the company, but for God's peace. I needed to take a step back and evaluate my true reason for working. Yes, it was to meet the needs of my family, but it was also to glorify the Lord. Taking this time to reflect on how I was feeling helped me move forward with not only a good attitude, it also kept me on track to best serve both the company and Christ. I understood perfectly that my first priority was to serve Christ wherever He placed me. I also knew that there was nothing wrong with knocking on doors in seeking better financial means to provide for my family. I just had to do so with a pure heart while maintaining a good attitude at my work place.

I then decided to further my education in hopes that it would help me advance in the company. I began attending IVY Tech Community College majoring in Business Administration with emphasis in Management. I completed roughly one year worth of classes by taking two classes each week during the evenings. This was when my manager decided to leave the department to expand his opportunities in another department. In his departure, he agreed that I should be made either a team lead or supervisor. The only thing holding me back then was that the new manager had not been hired. I decided to apply for that job. Why not? I knew everything there was to know about the warehouse.

Within two weeks of my applying for this new position, I was hit with news that rocked my world—Donna was arrested! She had developed compulsive behaviors that were due to addictions that were developed from the pain killers she was taking for her Cerebral Palsy. I clearly was not prepared for this. In trying to excel in my professional career, I was neglecting my family. I was working fifty hours and taking six hours of college classes each week. After adding the hours spent studying and sleeping, I was not spending much time with my family. I had this idea in my head that all my hard work was for them which justified the lack of time I had with them. Once again, I found my inability to balance my time properly with my family had negative consequences. This left me with little choice. I had to withdraw my name from the management position I was applying for. I also decided to withdraw from college to get my priorities back in order.

My employer found a well-qualified manager for the position. He worked like no other manager I had worked with in the company. He relieved much of the pressure on me due to his ability to focus on the work that needed done in the warehouse. It was becoming clear to me that the need for a team lead or supervisor was no longer needed. I met with him and he stated the same thing, but ensured me that as the company grew the need for this position would as well. So, here I am to this day holding out for this position to open up. I Trust that one day something will open up for me as I move forward in serving Christ, my family and my employer.

Although I have worked hard to maintain a good attitude, I understand why I have been dealt these cards. It was my doing years ago when I allowed myself to get caught up in sin that led to my felony. This felony to this day is still hanging over my head like a glass ceiling that I am not able to break. I am learning to be content with the fact that this ceiling may never break. Although, I still hold on to the principle that contentment does not mean you need to lose ambition to succeed. I trust with all my heart that the Lord wants us all to be content where He places us while at the same time seeking Him for further direction. I personally have left breaking that glass ceiling up to Christ.

Ch. 6

†

LIVING IN A GLASS HOUSE

This chapter is critical to understanding the full extent of living life as a registered sex offender. There is a price to pay to society that all registered sex offenders will have to face their entire lives. That debt is brought on by the severed trust created by the criminal actions of the sex offender. Therefore, it is reasonable to expect every sex offender that is released back into society to register with their local law enforcement agency. In the following paragraphs, I've utilized the information provided to me by the Vanderburgh County Sheriff's Department during the time of my registration on the Indiana Sex Offender Registry. It is easy to understand why I compared being a registered sex offender to living in a glass house.

According to the documents I received as a registered sex offender, there are many offenses that one can be charged with that leads to being classified as a registered sex offender: rape, criminal deviant conduct, child molestation, child exploitation, vicarious sexual gratification, child solicitation, child seduction, sexual misconduct with a minor (class A, B,

71

or C felony), incest, sexual battery, kidnapping or criminal confinement (if victim is less than eighteen years of age), possession of child pornography (if the person has a prior unrelated conviction of child pornography), an attempt or conspiracy to commit any of the crimes listed above.

There are two classifications placed on all registered sex offenders; there's the sex offender and the sexually violent predator. If the offender has been convicted of at least one sex offense when they were at least eighteen years of age and against a victim who was under the age of twelve at the time of the crime; or a sex offender committed a sex crime with aggravating circumstances, then they are classified as a sexually violent predator. In such cases, they are required to register as a sexually violent predator for the remainder of their lifetime. All other sex offenders are required to register for only ten years from their release date of incarceration.

Regardless of the length of time the offender is on the Sex Offender Registry, there are many rules that must be followed while on the registry. If these rules are not followed, the offender will be faced with an additional felony conviction and henceforth be returned to prison. Once registered as a sex offender, the offender's photo and personal information is placed on their local law enforcements registry. All the information related to their criminal conviction is included on this website as well. In Vanderburgh County there is a $50.00 annual fee for being on the registry which is expected at the point of registration.

All registered sex offenders must register every address where they may reside, attend school, work, or any real property owned. If there is a change to any of these addresses, or if any additional addresses have been obtained, the offender has three days to submit these changes to their local law enforcement agency. If at any period the registered sex offender plans to reside at any location in their county or any other county in the state for at least seven days out of any one hundred and eighty day period, they must register that address at their local law enforcement agency. All registered offenders are subject to random checks from their local law enforcement to validate any of the registered addresses.

The registered sex offender is not legally allowed to petition for a change of name. If the offender's name has been changed due to marriage, they have within thirty days to notify their local law enforcement agency. All registered sex offenders are required to obtain and keep on their possession a valid driver's license or state issued identification card issued by the state in which the sex offender resides. This proper identification must be shown each time the registered sex offender appears before their law enforcement agency to re-register.

As part of the registration requirements, sexually violent predators, who will be absent from their principle registered address for more than seventy-two hours, shall inform the local law enforcement authority. They must report that they will be absent from their principle address, they also must provide the address in which they will be located during their absence. They must also provide the time they will be absent from their principle address. If the new location is in a different county, the sexually violent offender must inform the local law enforcement authority in that county.

It is unlawful for a sexually violent offender to reside within one thousand feet of a school, a youth program center, or a public park. It's also prohibited for the offender to reside within one mile of the residence of the victim of the offender's sex offence. All registered sex offenders, regardless of status, must surrender all log-on information to any computer networking site they are a part of. Any computer owned or operated by the registered sex offender is subject to random checks by their local law enforcement agency to ensure that the log on information provided is accurate. All information obtained while being on the sex offender registry can be located and printed through this link, by clicking on the PDF link titled Sex Offenders who are required to register. (http://www.in.gov/idoc/reentry/files/Notification_Form_−_Duties_-_070108.pdf) [1.]

It is clear that the local law enforcement agency is keeping a close eye on the registered sex offenders in their area. The many rules and regulations have been set in place for the safety of the community in which the offender is living. The offender understands that their local law enforcement is watching their every move. They also are well aware that the community in which they live is also watching their every move. It is possible to live in such an environment. I did it for 14 years. It is far from easy, but it is better than living life behind bars. I am sure the severity of the offenders' charges heightens the consequences of the environment in which they live. Regardless of the details of one's past, if you're committed to a changed life through Christ, the faith in knowing Christ is in control of your destiny makes living in such an environment bearable. Through the power of the Holy Spirit, the individual living in this kind of environment can do so with peace and joy.

Ch. 7

†

BUTTERFLY EFFECT

The phrase "butterfly effect" refers to the idea that a butterfly's wings might create tiny changes in the atmosphere that may ultimately alter the path of a tornado or delay, accelerate or even prevent the occurrence of a tornado in a certain location. The flapping wing represents a small change in the initial condition of the system, which causes a chain of events leading to large-scale alterations of events. Had the butterfly not flapped its wings, the trajectory of the system might have been vastly different. Of course, the butterfly cannot literally cause a tornado. The kinetic energy in a tornado is enormously larger than the energy in the turbulence of a butterfly. The kinetic energy of a tornado is ultimately provided by the sun and the butterfly can only influence certain details of weather events in a chaotic manner. (http://dictionary.reference.com/browse/Butterfly+effect) [1.]

The theory that even the smallest step one takes in his/her life can change the course of said life immensely. The name of this theory came to be when a Chaos Theory stated: "It has been said that something as small as the flutter of a butterfly's wing can ultimately cause a typhoon halfway around the world." These choices, once chosen, are all examples of the Butterfly Effect and how one of these choices vs. another will affect one's life greatly. (http://www. urbandictionary.com/define.php?term=butterfly+effect) [2.]

Allow me to expound on this theory by stating that even the smallest step taken can affect the lives of those around you as well. It is easy for some people to continue indulging in their sinful behaviors when thinking they will be the only ones affected by their choices. It's clear that the indulgence of sin over a long period of time has largely affected our current state of morality today. Seriously, think about where we are as a nation morally. Everyday a story about a sexual-related charge is broadcast on one or more of the many news channels. The family watch-dog website has each state registered sex offenders totaled up numerically, as posted below in February 12, 2011.

State	Number of offenders	State	Number of offenders
California	64252	Iowa	5133
Texas	63171	Arkansas	4990
Florida	55707	Montana	4928
Michigan	45105	Arizona	4450
Ohio	27061	Idaho	3490
Illinois	24793	Nebraska	3465
Wisconsin	19943	West Virginia	3216

New York	18399	Nevada	3067
Virginia	17609	Delaware	2948
North Carolina	17221	Maine	2934
Tennessee	14994	Alaska	2764
Indiana	12965	South Dakota	2762
Missouri	12384	Massachusetts	2710
Pennsylvania	10708	Hawaii	2655
South Carolina	10570	New Jersey	2476
Louisiana	9795	New Mexico	2423
Georgia	9408	New Hampshire	2106
Alabama	8659	Wyoming	1444
Colorado	7649	Vermont	1375
Kansas	7452	District of Columbia	869
Maryland	7011	Oklahoma	822
Utah	6896	Oregon	708
Kentucky	6552	North Dakota	410
Mississippi	6359	Rhode Island	359
Washington	5969	Minnesota	231
Connecticut	5262	**Total Registered:**	**558,629**

This list contains the actual number of offenders that are publicly viewable in the official state registries. (http://www.familywatchdog.us/OffenderCountByState.asp) [3.]

I added the totals of offenders from each individual state, there are 558,629 people registered as sex offenders nationally. That means, with our current national population as of April 1st, 2010 estimated at 308,745,538, about 1 out of every 552 people is listed on a sex offender's registry in this country. (http://2010.census.gov/2010census/data/apportionment-data.php) [4.] This should illustrate that the choices made to continue in sexual sins has affected many people.

What brought us to where we are today? I do not think it was any one thing that dragged us down to where we currently find ourselves. I think it was the choices to commit some form of sexual sin that affected someone else in many ways. As these choices continued to be made by different individuals, many more individuals were affected by the consequences of these choices. The butterfly wings described in the butterfly effect is like the pattern of sexual sins that has continued from generation to generation—which has gradually grown into a storm of perversion. Now our country is dealing with the reality that we have 558,629 registered sex offenders living amongst us. This amount will no doubt climb as time progresses.

During my time in jail, I met many interesting individuals. I got to know a lot about their life stories as they opened up to me. All of these men were charged with a variety of sexual-related charges. Each dealt with their own individual upbringing that no doubt influenced the choices they made. I think their influences are important to illustrate the butterfly effect of sin in our society today. One man explained to me how his parents forced him to participate in child pornography. Another man shared with me how he was repeatedly assaulted by his priest. I had another man tell me how he was abandoned by his parents and passed from one foster home to another. In each home, he was molested on different occasions. Each of these men was seemingly stuck in the days of their abuse. Each time they spoke of the events that brought them to where they were, they would continually bring up the tragic events of their past.

The butterfly effect demonstrates how someone's past can have a dramatic impact on their future. I think this point is clear and understandable by all who consider the facts. The reality of this effect destroying lives is obvious, especially considering the current count of registered sex offenders. Anyone that has had their future devastated by acts they have committed due to their past should realize a very important truth. There is no doubt that someone's past can affect them dramatically, but it is important to realize that their present actions are performed solely by them and the responsibility falls on no one else. **"But every man is tempted, when he is drawn away of his own lust, and enticed. Then when lust hath conceived, it bringeth forth sin: and sin, when it is finished, bringeth forth death" (James 1: 14-15).** In order to truly repent of any sin committed, accepting responsibility for that sin must occur. There must be a true remorse from the heart that draws you to the Lord. **"Now I rejoice, not that ye were made sorry, but that ye sorrowed to repentance: for ye were made sorry after a Godly manner, that ye might receive damage by us in nothing. For Godly sorrow worketh repentance to salvation not to be repented of; but the sorrow of the world worketh death" (2 Corinthians 7: 9, 10).**

Living life is comparable to running a race. Both are performed best when you learn from your past experiences while being able to leave the weight of those experiences behind you in order to focus on what is in front of you. **"Wherefore seeing we also are compassed about with so great a cloud of witnesses, let us lay aside every weight, and the sin which doeth so easily beset us, and let us run with patience the race that is set before us" (Hebrews 12:1).** It is imperative to lay aside the tragedies that you may have experienced in the past. Otherwise, it is like trying to run a race carrying all the weight placed on you from those tragedies. It is crucial to be ready to forgive those that may have offended you. Doing so with the same forgiveness offered to you by Christ Himself, **"In whom we have redemption through His blood, the forgiveness of sins, according to the riches of His grace" (Ephesians 1:7).**

I have come to understand that just as dogs bark, because they are dogs, sinners will sin because they are sinners. **"The heart is deceitful above all things, and desperately wicked: who can know it?" (Jeremiah 17:9).** It is clear that if you have been offended; you will likely never forget what happened to you, but possessing the spirit of forgiveness will free you from much bitterness and strife. Through applying Christ-like forgiveness, the weights of bitterness will be taken from you. It is good to remember how Christ responded to those that crucified Him—He forgave them, **"Then said Jesus, Father, forgive them; for they know not what they do,** and they parted His raiment, and cast lots" (Luke 23:34). Why did Christ set this example? He knew that through His Holy Spirit that He could do the same through our lives. **"To open their eyes, and to turn them from darkness to light, and from the power of Satan unto God, that they may receive forgiveness of sins, and inheritance among them which are sanctified by faith that is in me"** (Acts 26:18). As much as society may hate those registered as sex offenders, Christ wants us to see them as sinners that need a Savior. It's important to remember that we, too, have need of a Savior to forgive our sins. It is good to hate their sins as we should hate our own sins, but through the strength of the Holy Spirit we need to make every attempt to reach out to them with the message of love through Christ.

This raises a series of questions that need to be resolved within every church. Are we prepared to meet the spiritual needs of the sex offender who has repented? How should we deal with the security issues? Should we tell our members if the sex offender continues to attend our church? What steps should we take to ensure the offender is being held accountable? These are questions that we should be focusing on, but in reality the questions first crossing the minds of most churches is: Do we really want sex offenders attending our church? After all, if they are discovered, it is likely that those discovering them may quit attending. All of these questions are reasonable. Therefore, I think it's important to spend a little time opening the debate on these questions in hopes that a resolution can be found.

Let's deal with the most obvious question first: Do we really want sex offender's attending our church? Well, that clearly depends on each church's capability to manage the responsibility required in having them there. There is a higher level of accountability that needs to be given to any sex offender. This is needed to ensure the safety of everyone within the church, at least until the individual in question has had time to prove that he or she has changed.

What steps should we take to ensure that the offender attending our church is being held accountable? After speaking to several churches and doing solid research on this issue, I've discovered some interesting ways of meeting this level of accountability. First and foremost, the most common method was to have a mentor assigned to the individual on the registry. The mentor is usually a deacon or faithful layman within the membership of the church. The mentor's responsibility would be to develop a bond of Christ-like love with the offender. In some churches, the offender is required to remain with their mentor at all times while on church property. In other churches the mentor is expected to only supervise the individual. The time-line of having a mentor assigned to the offender varied from church to church. They all agreed, though, that at some point the mentor would no longer be required.

It's also reasonable to expect the registered sex offender to adhere to a list of guidelines laid out by the leadership of the church. The objective of these guidelines should be set in place to not only ensure the safety of other members within the church, but also to protect the offender in his or her pursuit toward a relationship with Christ. These guidelines should be properly communicated to both the offender and their mentor. The consequences of not abiding by these guidelines should also be clearly laid out. Some of the requirements I have found in my research that have made the list of guidelines are as followed:

> The offender is to avoid any services with the focus being to minister to children.
> The offender is to avoid any sections of the building where children are present.
> The offender is to avoid any form of communication with children of any age or persons of the opposite sex, as to avoid the appearance of evil.
> The offender is to participate in some form of disciple-ship program with their mentor.

It is important to remember that not only are there offenders in the church, but there are also victims. This will clearly make it difficult for the two to unite in fellowship. This truly magnifies the importance for the pastoral staff to develop close relationships with the people God has placed under them. This bond is needed to open the door to learn information such as this—the balancing act of dealing with both spectrums of this issue can only be done if everyone involved is standing at the foot of the cross. While standing there we're all reminded that this is where we all have to be to both receive and to give the gift of forgiveness that is found in Jesus Christ.

If we are to effectively overcome this storm of sin that has overwhelmed our country, the church is going to have to get involved. Our country is quickly approaching 600,000 registered sex offenders. That not only reflects those who has been devastated by the sickness of sin, but it also sheds light on how many individuals have been unjustly victimized. I'm convinced that Christ has called me to reach out to the sex offenders in this county. I strongly believe that Christ can transform the lives of these individuals, just as Christ has transformed my life, through psychological counseling, the power of His Spirit, the leading of His Word and the presence of His grace.

Ch. 8

†

LIVING IN GRACE

Living in God's grace is something all Christians are equipped to do through the power of the Holy Spirit. It takes a relationship with Christ through His Word in order to live in His grace. This is why so many Christians are not enjoying the true freedom of living in God's grace. In today's society there are too many Christians walking in religion, instead of working to establish a relationship with Christ through His Word. It is easier to follow the different rules that we think are set up by our church leadership especially if those rules make us feel more Christ-like. The mind set of being religious has turned biblical principles into rules that we feel we must live by. This mindset has led to the lie many believe that if they abide by these rules they are living right with God and therefore have earned His grace.

It is important to understand the meaning of grace. The definition alone removes any possibility of earning it. Grace is defined as, "free and unmerited favor of God". Some individuals even assume that favor with God is *earned* when praying a prayer to accept Christ as their personal

Savior. This is not the case either. It's true that salvation comes by grace through faith. **"For by grace are ye saved through faith; and that not of yourselves; it is the gift of God: Not of works, lest any man should boast" (Ephesians 2:8-9).** This verse clearly points out that grace and faith are both required to reach salvation. It is clear that grace is given to us by God. The definition itself shows that. Some believe that the measure of faith required to reach salvation is something we do. This simply is not true. Faith in Christ comes through the hearing of God's Word, **"So then faith cometh by hearing, and hearing by the Word of God" (Romans 10:17).** As well as the Holy Spirit working in our hearts, **". . . no man can say that Jesus is the Lord, but by the Holy Ghost" (I Cor. 12:3).** The power of God's Word and the conviction of the Holy Spirit in your heart and mind is when true salvation occurs. It's important to understand that this has nothing to do with what you may have done in the process.

We should all be careful to be sure we are properly witnessing for Christ. Many individuals can go through life thinking they are saved by simply praying a prayer of salvation. That prayer can become a work if that prayer alone is what is relied on to receive salvation. There is nothing we can do within ourselves to profess Jesus is Lord; it takes the moving of the Holy Spirit in our hearts to do that. When the truth of Christ's death, burial and resurrection is presented to us through God's Word, and the Holy Spirit draws our heart to the faith required to accept this truth, our spirit is then regenerated by the Spirit of God. At that point we are new creatures, **"Therefore if any man be in Christ, he is a new creature: old things are passed away; behold, all things are become new" (2 Cor. 5:17)**.

So, what exactly has become new in the new believer's life at this point? The remnant of who we once were is still present. Therefore, if left to ourselves, our wicked, sinful heart would fall right back into the sins that we once desired. Thankfully, we are not left to ourselves. The Holy Spirit of God that brought us to the point of accepting Christ as our savior did not leave us after that point. Instead, from that point forward He has dwelt in us, providing us the power and strength to overcome any sin that our wicked heart may desire. **"That He would grant you, according to the riches of His glory, to be strengthened with might by His Spirit in the inner man" (Eph. 3:16)**. The power and strength through the Holy Spirit is available for every Christian to draw upon. A personal relationship with Christ must be developed to do this, though. This is where my problem initially began. I was living a life of religion and not walking daily in a relationship with Christ.

The Holy Spirit performs His good work in every believer on a daily basis, diligently working to mold us into the person Christ desires us to be. This work begins by exposing what is truly in our hearts. The Holy Spirit used the Word of God along with the choices I made to expose what was really in my heart. As the wickedness in my heart was exposed, I turned my heart over to God for forgiveness. **"Repent therefore of this thy wickedness, and pray God, if perhaps the thought of thine heart may be forgiven thee" (Acts 8:22).** God's grace is most prevalent in the working of His Spirit in our hearts. It is His purpose to strengthen our mortal bodies to overcome the weakness of our flesh. **"But if the Spirit of Him that raised up Jesus from the dead dwell in you, He that raised up Christ from the dead shall also quicken your mortal bodies by His Spirit that dwelleth in you" (Romans 8:11).**

Donna and I are perfect examples of how the Holy Spirit will continue the work which He had begun after we opened our hearts to salvation. The Lord used Donna's physical ailments many years ago to expose my wicked, self-centered heart. He then used His Word, along with the circumstances surrounding the consequences we had to face, to continue working in our hearts. As you have read throughout this book, the Lord never stopped working in our lives. His faithfulness had brought us through much hardship. We have come to the understanding that truly living in God's grace means to rely on Him for everything; because within ourselves, our righteousness is as filthy rags. **"But we are all as an unclean thing, and all our righteousnesses are as filthy rags" (Isaiah 64:6).**

Donna went through many valleys in her life as well in which God's grace abounded much. About midway through the year 2005, her mother lost her battle with cancer. The pain that Donna felt due to this loss was overwhelming. At the time of her mother's death, Donna was already dealing with her lifelong struggle of Cerebral Palsy. The pain medication that was being given to her for this problem was quickly found to greatly assist her with the emotional grief she was dealing with. Clearly her physician could only give her a limited amount, which was not what she felt she needed to get through her grief; so, she sought additional physicians to get her hands on more. This was all being done outside of my knowledge. I was busy working fifty hours a week while attending college courses during the evenings for an additional six hours each week.

Considering this lifelong disability my wife had to deal with, I should have educated myself more about the details of her situation. It would have greatly helped in knowing what warning signs to look out for during the loss of her mother. All I noticed was that during the time I was spending with her she seemed happy and content. Her absence of grief should have been my first warning sign. Unfortunately, we were seldom around one another due to work and college. I eventually came to the realization that every time I was around her; she was high on prescription pain medication. When I questioned her about it, she shared that they helped her with everything she was dealing with. I was ignorant about the dangers of addiction to prescription drugs, so I brushed the issue off thinking she needed the extra help that these prescriptions were giving her.

I later received a phone call informing me that Donna was in jail. I just sat down and cried. I placed all the blame on myself. Being the spiritual leader of my home, I knew I had failed my wife. I should have never allowed my desire to advance at my place of employment to keep me away from my family. I should have done more to educate myself with the danger of addictions. My selfishness to excel at my place of employment consumed much of my time. I am sure that Donna never dreamed this addiction would take her to jail. It was reasonable to think that after all we have been through that she would have known exactly where sin would take her. It is clear that sin has a way of blinding the individual overtaken in sin when they fail to utilize the power they have been given through the Holy Spirit to overcome their sin. **"For a just man falleth seven times, and riseth up again: but the wicked shall fall into mischief" (Proverbs 24:16).**

The recovery process that Donna had to endure was an extensive struggle, and our whole family felt the pressure. The powerful components in the drug Hydrocodone were very addictive. They created compulsive behaviors in Donna that led to her arrest. The nights of detoxing seemed endless. Both physical and mental anguish took control of her very being. Going through this was not an easy experience. Neither of us expected the consequences that came from cleansing her body and mind of this powerful drug. It was clear that the Lord was using the many circumstances in Donna's life to continue the work in her heart to make her into what Christ desired her to be. The power of His grace is what saw us through the darkest nights brought on by this addiction. **"Now no chastening for the present seemeth to be joyous, but grievous: nevertheless afterward it yieldeth the peaceable fruit of righteousness unto them which are exercised thereby"** (Hebrews 12:11).

The circumstances surrounding Donna's addiction was used to clean up her life. It was also used to get my priorities back on track. My first priority was getting my family back on track spiritually. Both she and I took full responsibility for our own wrong doing. Donna understood very clearly that the set of circumstances that she had to deal with was not a justification for what she did. They were used to expose what was truly in her heart, so that the Holy Spirit could continue His work. **"Being confident of this very thing, that He which hath a begun a good work in you will perform it until the day of Jesus Christ"** (Philippians 1:6). Donna realized that instead of relying on the Lord to comfort her through her circumstances, she resorted back to the things that comforted her in her youth. Her comfort was through substance abuse and the artificial strength that arises from the use of it. That strength is temporal. It only lasts while you are under its influence. This further explains the compulsive behavior in the flesh that draws the user to seek further consumption. True lasting strength comes only through the Holy Spirit and by living in His grace.

The Lord uses circumstances in our lives to reveal Himself to us in many ways. Each time Christ is revealed to us, it strengthens our spirit to continue pressing on. I recall my last experience when this occurred to me. This occurred during my sixth week into the Celebrate Recovery Inside group, I volunteered at in the county jail. I was feeling down and discouraged due to a variety of reasons both at home and at work. I went into the jail prepared to teach my first lesson after weeks of training. When I got there, the chaplain informed me that the guy I have been training with was not going to be there. So, he wanted me to go into the other two cell blocks with one of the volunteers. I always try to stay sensitive to the moving of the Lord, so I chose to remain silent about the lesson I came prepared to share. As I went into the other cell blocks, I saw an inmate in there that made a comment to me. He said, "You again, I keep running into you." I looked at him puzzled. I did not have a clue as to who he was. Then after the session was over, he revealed to me who he was. He was the inmate that I witnessed accept Christ years ago when I was in jail. I felt goose bumps roll up my arm! I knew at that very moment that I was exactly where I was supposed to be. The Lord worked out all the details for me to be in this cell block in order to see this man again. The Lord knew what was going on in this man's life. It was the Lord's intent for me to do what I could to encourage this man. I did this with a new sense of strength that I so desperately needed.

Living in grace is being sensitive to the leading of the Holy Spirit. This is when you know that your heart is wickedly deceitful, and no man can know Christ without the

Holy Spirit. Living in grace knows that everything you have is from God and realizing the difference between a need and a want. It is living through the strength of the Holy Spirit and not on your own. You must come to the realization that your strength will not last in the time of need without Christ in your life. **"That He would grant you, according to the riches of His glory, to be strengthened with might by His Spirit in the inner man . . ." (Ephesians 3:16).** Living in God's grace changes you from within; it changes your character . . . **"But the fruit of the Spirit is love, joy, peace, longsuffering, gentleness, goodness, faith, Meekness, temperance: against such there is no law" (Galatians 5:22-23).**

Living in grace is more than just living for God in ways that will affect your life positively. It is about using what the Lord has taught you to affect the lives of others. If we are truly at a place in our lives where we know our hearts are wicked and deceitful, then shouldn't we do more to fulfill Gods' commandment to exhort one another? **"But exhort one another daily, while it is called today; lest any of you be hardened through the deceitfulness of sin" (Hebrews 3:13).** The grace of the Lord has been extended to all mankind. It is because of our sins that we need a Savior. **"For the grace of God that bringeth salvation hath appeared to all men" (Titus 2:11).** It is my goal to share my Savior to others in hopes that the Holy Spirit will open their hearts and minds to their need of Him.

Ch. 9

†

BONDAGE TO FREEDOM

Bondage can mean a few things as defined by the Webster dictionary: 1. the tenure or service of a villein, serf, or slave 2. A state of being bound, by compulsion (as of law or mastery): as a: CAPTIVITY, SERFDOM b: servitude or subjugation to a controlling person or force young people in bondage to drugs 3. Sadomasochistic sexual practices involving the physical restraint of one partner. (http://www.merriam-webster.com/dictionary/bondage) [1.] The form of bondage I will be referring to is one's tenure or service as a slave, as well as the compulsive behavior of the addict under subjugation to a controlling force.

During my journey through all this, I have learned that the bondage of compulsive or addictive behavior destroys lives. Allowing yourself to be controlled by the compulsive behavior of the flesh that comes with an addiction is no different than allowing an evil spirit to direct your life. It controls the way you feel each day and the way you treat others. It controls how you manage your finances, your time and how you make decisions throughout your life.

These compulsions control everything about you. You're happy when you are experiencing the high they give you and depressed when you are not. There is so much to get addicted to today such as: alcohol, marijuana, tobacco, prescription drugs, meth, heroin, pornography and etc. All of these substances will take complete control of you both physically and mentally. I have experienced the power of these compulsions. The stronger these urges are, the more in bondage you feel.

I allowed myself to be controlled by pornography that took me places I never dreamed I would go. As you have read in this book, it took a long journey for me to regain control of my life. The stages of my personal recovery began with accepting responsibility for my behavior without blaming it on other people or my childhood. I then established personal boundaries by mentally setting up red flags at locations that I knew would only cause me to fall. I faithfully attended church while working diligently to establish a ministry networking our members together for exhortation. I disciplined myself to get into God's Word daily and to establish a heart of constant prayer. These are steps that I learned through my pastor. I can verify that they work wonderfully. I could have chosen my own route, but I truly wanted to regain control of my life. God's Word would always pound in my heart during these challenging times, **"All things are lawful unto me, but all things are not expedient: all things are lawful for me, but I will not be brought under the power of any"** (1 Corinthians 6:12).

Regaining control of my life was essential in getting my family back. God's Word states, **"Good understanding giveth favour: but the way of transgressors is hard" (Proverbs 13:15)**. It was clear to me that a life lived with Christ and for Christ to serve others was a life worth living. I attempted the self-centered route and was met only with hardship and heartbreak. The more I began to develop a closer relationship to God, the more possible I felt it was to get my name removed from the Sex Offender Registry. I asked the Corporal in charge of the registry at the sheriff's office if anyone has ever been removed from the list. He said, "No, the only way that could occur is if the court ordered it." So, I began praying fervently for the Lord to open up a door for this to occur.

When my tenth year on the registry passed, I was sick at my stomach. According to my plea deal, that was the year I was supposed to be done registering. The Legislature amended the Indiana Code regarding registry requirements, which stopped that from occurring. That amendment requires lifetime registration for a defendant whose offence qualifies the defendant as a "sexually violent predator". Both before and after this amendment, "sexually violent predator" was defined as a person who suffers from a mental abnormality or personality disorder that makes the individual likely to repeatedly commit sex offenses.
(http://www.in.gov/legislative/ic/code/title11/ar8/ch8.html) [2.]

I knew with all my heart that I would never repeat my sinful actions of my past. After much time in prayer, I sought an attorney to assist me with my case. There was no doubt that God was at work because I did not have much money to pay an attorney. The attorney I found was a friend of my sister. Therefore, I received an excellent financial deal. He was very detailed and wanted to make sure all of our bases were covered. He communicated with both my wife and my victim and retrieved signed affidavits concerning the details of my case. The more powerful of these two was the one that stated I never physically touched my victim. My reasoning for my appeal was for three purposes: (1) the Act violates the ex post facto provisions of both the Indiana and federal Constitutions, (2) the Act violates my rights to life, liberty, and the pursuit of happiness under the State and federal Constitutions, and (3) my plea agreement should be rendered involuntary because I was not advised that I would be required to register for life as a sex offender.

My attorney went to court with all of his guns loaded. He was prepared for every angle. He was confident my case violated the ex post facto provisions in the Constitutions and that, within itself, should be just cause to consider my case as time served and therefore remove my information from the registry. When we went to court, the judge, prosecutor and my attorney decided to discuss this issue in private in the judge's chambers. I was told by him that he would call me with a response as soon as he got it. I went back to work which seemed like one of the longest days of my life. A few hours later the phone rang. My heart began pounding in desperation to know what was determined with my case. My attorney sounded exhilarated. He stated, "We did it!" I just stood there, waiting for him to expound on that phrase. Then he said, "We got you off the internet; you no longer will be on the Registry." I said, "Will I be deleted from the site?" He said, "As soon as the required paperwork makes it to the Sheriff's Department." I was stunned, it was finally over! It was like a ton of weights being lifted off my shoulders. I sincerely felt as light as a feather.

I fell to my knees in tears crying to the Lord with thanksgiving. He has been so faithful to me throughout this whole ordeal, I felt like I owed him so much. First, He freed me from the bondage of pornography. Then He freed me from the bondage of being on the Sex Offender Registry. I realized I still had my felony conviction hanging over my head; but being deleted off the Registry completely was a monumental step in the right direction. It is now my hopes to one day have my charges reduced, or even dropped altogether. I have placed that process in the hands of the Lord. He has faithfully worked things out. I trust in His time that this will come to pass as well.

It is amazing to experience the freedom that comes through the grace of God. This freedom can be experienced regardless of the level of consequences you may be enduring due to the choices you made in your past. I encourage you to get into God's Word daily, seek after the Lord with all your heart, soul and mind; he will reveal himself to you. **"Yea, if thou criest after knowledge, and liftest up thy voice for understanding; If thou seekest her as silver, and searchest for her as for hid treasures; Then shalt thou understand the fear of the LORD, and find the knowledge of God"** (Proverbs 2:3-5).

In order to experience true freedom from bondage, it has to come through the blood of Christ by faith. **"But if we walk in the light, as He is in the light, we have fellowship one with another, and the blood of Jesus Christ His Son cleanseth us from all sin"** (1John 1:7). Christ Jesus loves everyone; He desires for none to perish. **"The Lord is not slack concerning His promise, as some men count slackness; but is longsuffering to us-ward, not willing that any should perish, but that all should come to repentance"** (2Peter 3:9). Due to our continued sins, we deserve to perish in hell for eternity **"For the wages of sin is death, but the gift of God is eternal life through Jesus Christ our Lord"** (Romans 6:23). The love that Christ has for us is proven in His death **"But God commendeth His love toward us, in that, while we were yet sinners, Christ died for us"** (Romans 5:8). The death of Christ is all the payment required for our sins. All we need to do is accept that payment **"That if thou shalt confess with thy mouth the Lord Jesus, and shalt believe in thine heart that God hath raised Him from the dead, thou shalt be saved. For with the heart man believeth unto righteousness; and with the mouth confession is made unto salvation"** (Romans 10:9-10).

God's gift of salvation has been made complete in the sacrifice made by Christ. All we need to do is by faith accept that gift of grace by calling on Christ to be our Lord and Savior. We are to continue living in God's grace by faith knowing He has freed us from the bondage of sin. This freedom comes by the power of the Holy Spirit who set up residence in our inner man once we have accepted Christ. **"That He would grant you, according to the riches of His glory, to be strengthened with might by His Spirit in the inner man" (Ephesians 3:16).**

In receiving Christ, we can rest in the fact that He is with us always, working out the intimate details of our lives. **"Therefore take no thought, saying, What shall we eat? or, What shall we drink? or, Wherewithal shall we be clothed? (For after all these things do the Gentiles seek :) for your heavenly Father knoweth that ye have need of all these things" (Matt. 6:31-32).** To truly experience the freedom in Christ, we must rely on Him for everything. When everything is falling down around us, the strength of Christ will see us through. We stand trusting in Him continually as we press on toward a life of perseverance. God's Word promises to everyone that waits on the Lord that He will renew their strength. **"But they that wait upon the LORD shall renew their strength; they shall mount up with wings as eagles; they shall run, and not be weary; and they shall walk, and not faint" (Isaiah 40:31).**

WORKS CITED

✝

Chapter 1

1. Rosenberg & Associates, Victims of sexual abuse, 2006,
    http://www.aaets.org/article123.htm
    (Accessed June 13, 2010).

Chapter 6

1. In.gov website, http://www.in.gov/idoc/reentry/2505.htm,
    Sex and Violent Offender Registration Responsibilities
    and Other Duties
    http://www.in.gov/idoc/reentry/files/Notification
    Form—Duties - 070108.pdf, Printable PDF file,
    (Accessed Nov. 1st, 2010)

Chapter 7

1. Butterfly effect encyclopedia topics | Reference.com
    http://dictionary.reference.com/browse/Butterfly+effect
    (Accessed June 13, 2010)

2. Urban Dictionary: butterfly effect, Example No. 3
    http://www.urbandictionary.com/define.php?term=
    butterfly+effect
    (Accessed June 13, 2010)

3. Family watch dog, Offender Count
    http://www.familywatchdog.us/OffenderCountByState.asp
    (Accessed February 12, 2011)

4. U.S Census 2010, Apportionment Data
    http://2010.census.gov/2010census/data/apportionment-
    data.php
    (Accessed February 12, 2011)

Chapter 9

1. Bondage—Definition and More from the Free Merriam-
    Webster Dictionary
    http://www.merriam-webster.com/dictionary/bondage
    (Accessed June 13, 2010)

2. Indiana Code 11-8-8-19, Expiration of duty to register;
    lifetime registration; out-of-state registrants
    http://www.in.gov/legislative/ic/code/title11/ar8/ch8.html
    (Accessed Nov. 1st, 2010)